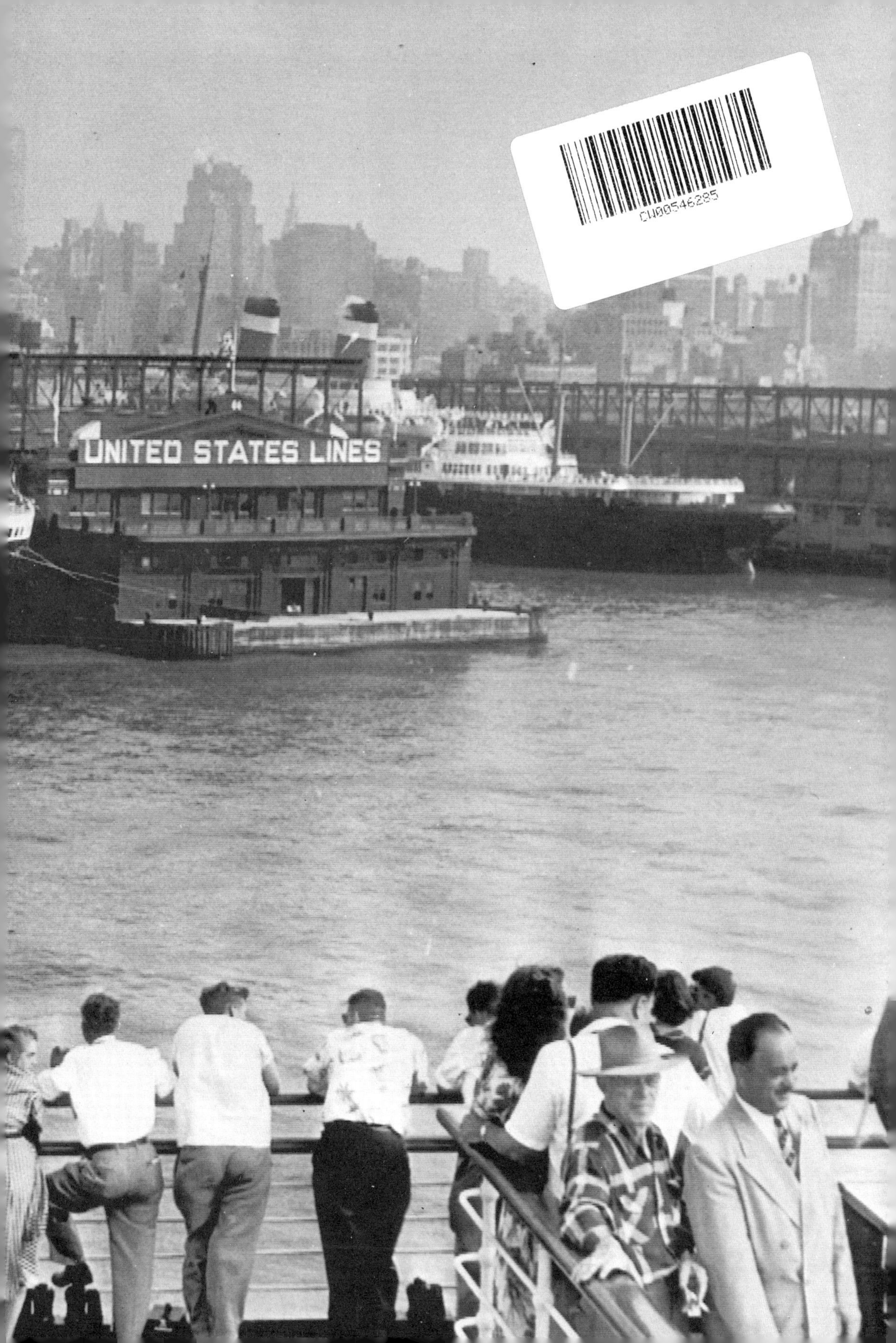
UNITED STATES LINES

SS United States

SS United
States

The story of America's greatest ocean liner

William H. Miller

Foreword by Margaret Truman Daniel

PSL

Patrick Stephens Limited

First published 1991

British Library Cataloguing in Publication Data
Miller, William H.
SS United States: the story of America's greatest ocean liner.
1. Passenger transport. Shipping. Steam liners. (Ship)
United States, history
I. Title
387.2432

ISBN 1-85260-204-X

Front endpaper A once familiar sight: the *United States* at New
York's 'Luxury Liner Row', as viewed from the deck of the
outbound *Queen Elizabeth* and with the *Constitution* also at berth.
(*Frank O. Braynard Collection*)

Title page Sailing at noon from New York's West Side piers: the
United States is in the centre, the *Constitution* is on the left, and the
stern of the *America* on the right. (*Flying Camera Inc*)

Patrick Stephens Limited, a subsidiary of the Haynes Publishing
Group P.L.C., has published authoritative, quality books for
enthusiasts for more than twenty years. During that time the
company has established a reputation as one of the world's leading
publishers of books on aviation, maritime, military, model-making,
motor cycling, motoring, motor racing, railway and railway modelling
subjects. Readers or authors with suggestions for books they would
like to see published are invited to write to: The Editorial Director,
Patrick Stephens Limited, Haynes Publishing Group P.L.C.,
Sparkford, Nr Yeovil, Somerset BA22 7JJ.

Printed in Great Britain
Typesetting by MJL Limited, Hitchin, Hertfordshire

1 3 5 7 9 10 8 6 4 2

This book is for

ELIZABETH D. ALEXANDERSON

'The power behind the throne'

Contents

Opposite The loudest whistles in all of New York harbour signal another noontime departure for Europe. (*Frank O. Braynard Collection*)

Foreword
by Margaret Truman Daniel

When it comes to ships, I have had two loves in my life. One was the *USS Missouri*, a great battleship that I christened with the name of my home state during the Second World War. And the other was the *SS United States*, in which I sailed on the fastest voyage ever made across the Atlantic Ocean in 1952. The trip lasted 3 days, 10 hours and 40 minutes. That record won the coveted Blue Riband, not held by the USA in a century. The speed of that crossing has never been exceeded, and may very well stand forever because they don't make trans-oceanic liners like the *United States* anymore.

Nothing in my then-young life could have been more exciting than the moment when the record was set. I was travelling to England on the maiden voyage of the *United States* with my dear friend—then and now—Drucie Horton. She was the daughter of the Secretary of the Treasury in the cabinet of my father, President Truman. The captain of the *United States* on that historic voyage was Commodore Harry Manning.

He invited us junior VIPs to join him on the bridge at the climax of the voyage. He warned us to dress warmly (not just in our evening wraps) because it would be cold on the bridge. It was indeed cold, and the land coming into view was shrouded in a damp fog typical of England. When we passed Bishop's Rock, marking the end of the transatlantic crossing, we couldn't even see it. We saw its blip on the radar. The elapsed time of the crossing, while made at very high speed, was not at the maximum of which the *United States* was capable. I've never been so thrilled in all my life.

In fact, it was always thrilling to cross on the *United States*, with her trim lines, her sleek hull, her steadiness, and the power throbbing from her engines. I made two more crossings on the ship, one with Commodore Leroy Alexanderson in command. Then, my romance with the *United States* unhappily ended. She sails the seas no more.

Opposite Moran tugs guide the *Big U* into the Hudson. The stern of the Greek *Olympia* is on the left; the *America* is on the right, still berthed at Pier 86. (*Frank O. Braynard Collection*)

Acknowledgements

A great many people have been extraordinarily generous in helping me write this book, in sharing letters and files, cherished mementoes and well-preserved newspaper clippings, and in spending time talking about the SS *United States*. I have also been given enormous support and encouragement, which is especially important to any writer for there are often mountains to climb and hurdles to overcome.

Commodore Alexanderson and his wife Elizabeth were, of course, the absolute primary sources of this book, and certainly its inspiration. I spent so many wonderful days at their home in Virginia, touring the ship and the shipyards and other related facilities, and of course benefitting from their many introductions. With Elizabeth's guiding force, we moved forward with the Commodore's recollections, often well into the night. And then, quite often, early on the very next morning, the Commodore would climb to their attic and retrieve yet more ageing photographs and yellowing newsclips. Always, they were wonderful to work with.

I was also very fortunate in locating a splendid team that worked aboard and sailed the *Big U*. Nick Bachko has a brilliant knowledge of the ship. Les Barton, the former chief quartermaster, spoke with great intimacy as well. His apartment, along New York City's Upper West Side, also contained cherished memorabilia from the liner. Captain Bob Brooks shared his impressions and Dave Fitzgerald, also a treasure chest of recollections, has the added bonus of living on the New Jersey shore of the Hudson River, directly opposite Pier 86 where the *Big U* berthed. Al Grant shared not only his remembrances, but contacted others as well. While some contacts were made by 'phone, such as with Ed Macy, Marge Marshall recounted her *United States* sailing days over a Saturday lunch in the delightful setting of

Opposite Commodore Leroy J. Alexanderson, the last master with that rank within the US passenger fleet, aboard the *United States*, the last Blue Riband holder on the Atlantic. (*Alexanderson Collection*)

her Long Island garden. Captain John Tucker, another master of the liner, offered his recollections as well.

Individuals at various organizations also helped: Sharon Davis Freeman at the Arthur Polizos Associates, Flying Camera Inc., Tom Crew and Bill Wilkinson at The Mariners' Museum, Moran Towing & Transportation Co., Jack A. Garrow, Lyn Lyon, J.E. Turner, Jr., Phyllis Stephenson and Gene Yaeger at the Newport News Shipbuilding & Dry Dock Company, Norshipco, the Port Authority of New York & New Jersey, United States Lines, and the United States Navy.

Three other individuals who were notably important in helping to create this book were Frank Duffy, Bill Fox, and Dr Robert L. Scheina. Ocean liner historians, collectors, and maritime buffs were inevitably helpful, supportive, and sharing: Michael Aronson, Dietmar Borchert, Frank Braynard, Philippe Brebant, Mark Carbinero, George Devol, Alex Duncan, Peter Fraser, John Geary, Bill Green, Bob Lenzer, John Maxtone-Graham, Fred Rodriguez, Bob Russell, Ken Schultz, Antonio Scrimali, Michael Shernoff, Everett Viez, Ed Wolcott, and Tim Yoder. Also very special thanks to Mrs Vincent Astor, Greg Daugherty, Dr Sarah E. Forbes, Joan Fox, and Mel Williams. And should there be any oversights, my obvious regrets; but rest assured that your help has been appreciated.

William H. Miller

I would be remiss if I did not acknowledge the help that I have received to make my career and this book possible. My wife, Elizabeth, was the inspiration for this book and pushed it along from beginning to end. My friend Bill Fox offered editorial assistance and a lot of encouragement. Bill Miller deserves thanks for his perseverance and patience, and for producing this fine book. I am also grateful to all of the officers of the Navy and the United States Lines who helped me during my career and in the preparation of this book.

It is said that in a foxhole, there are no atheists, and I believe it is also so on the bridge of a ship. When going into any port or travelling in dense fog, one must have faith, and there is always someone at my side.

Commodore Leroy J. Alexanderson

Introduction

In the early darkness of a Tuesday night, 7 November 1969, the superliner *United States* slipped out of her berth at the foot of New York's West 46th Street. After hundreds of visits, those once customary three- and four-day layovers, that great ship would never again return to her homeport. She sailed without notation. It was merely to be a visit to her birthplace in Virginia for her annual overhaul. She was expected to return within a month's time, to sail on a Christmas cruise to the sunny waters of the Caribbean. Consequently, she sailed off with very little notice—without passengers, reduced staff, and barely any onlookers.

In about five weeks, as so many thought and confidently so, her full staff would return, along with about 1200 passengers, and she would steam off—away from the cold, often desolate, money-losing North Atlantic run—to the tropics, to the cherished warmth and sunshine, the shopping and swimming, of the Caribbean isles. Afterwards, in January, she would embark on her longest and perhaps grandest voyage ever: eight weeks and, for the first time in her career, into the Pacific. Bulky pieces of luggage, including many of those well-known steamer trunks, had already been delivered to Pier 86 in Manhattan and were being stored. Sadly, they would never go aboard.

The good times, those halcyon days, of fun and profit had become just fun for the world's fastest liner, one of the greatest of all passenger ships and certainly the most technologically advanced ever to sail under the Stars and Stripes. When built in the early 1950s, she was the ultimate symbol of Yankee genius, the seagoing centrepiece of post-war industrial might. She swept across the North Atlantic in the summer of 1952, breaking all records, and snatching the prized distinction of becoming Blue Riband champion from Britain's *Queen Mary*. With her huge red, white, and blue winged funnels, her long, low hull, and her silver-coated fittings, she sparkled in that first gloriously triumphant summer. Perhaps no other passenger ship since has equalled that radiance. She was front-page news, the star of newsreels, a household name. Everyone wanted to sail in her—or, at the very least, tour her innards. She appeared on magazine covers, toys were created in her likeness, and even Hollywood took an interest. For her first decade, she was the most popular single superliner on the Atlantic run. This appeal, this extraordinary fascination, was not restricted, however, to America; it was the same in Britain (her loudest maiden voyage reception was at Southampton) and continental Europe. Shippers and marine designers, the downtown shipping men, travel agents and potential travellers, and little boys (not matter what age!) who were entranced by great ships and the sea all made special excursions to waterfronts just to see her.

In my case, I remember her especially at New York, docked along 'Luxury Liner Row'. She always used Pier 86, mostly in the north slip, but very occasionally on the south side. Few liners could equal her exceptional size, particularly those extraordinary (and extremely modern, for their day) funnels. Only the French *Liberté* and later the *France*, and, of course, the Cunard *Queens* could equal her in height—those top decks, masts, and funnels seemingly resting atop the pier rooftops. In that age when the general public seemed more interested, more genuinely fascinated by those ocean-going marvels, the *United States* also often featured in those impromptu but glamorous and memorable collections of the world's greatest ocean liners gathered along Manhattan's West Side. At least two City newspapers, the *Daily News* and the long defunct *Daily Mirror*, often featured centrefold photos, usually aerial views, of these gatherings of luxury ships. There might be the likes of the *Constitution* or *Independence*, a Frenchman, possibly the Greek *Olympia* or *New York*, certainly two or more Cunarders, and, of course, very often the *America*, the fleetmate, the consort, the side-kick, if you will, of the *United States*. (Perhaps 'baby sister' is even appropriate.) Most noticeably, the funnels of these two United States Lines's passenger ships were similar, and when they were berthed together, sharing the same 1100-ft-long finger pier at West 46th Street, the similarity, the shared evolution of the two ships, was apparent. The night scenes were particularly evocative: alluring and glittering, with a touch of fantasy about them. Neat little white lights marked the decks while special floodlights gave a soft glow that accentuated the funnel colours.

But as the *Big U*—as she was widely and affectionately known—sailed out of New York on that darkening autumn evening in 1969, so much had already changed. The cast to which she belonged—and in a starring role—had been altered and reduced almost beyond recognition. The Cunard *Queens*, as examples, were gone—killed off by the abrupt technological intrusion of the jet aircraft. Almost immediately, in the late 1950s and continuing, perhaps even more forcefully, into the following decade, there was the inevitable defection of legions of travellers to the airports and a swifter if far less graceful mode of transport. Europe was six hours rather than six days away! Even the beloved *America* had gone, having been sold to the Greeks to ferry immigrants from their European homes to new lives that began at the docks of Melbourne, Sydney, and Auckland. The *Constitution* and *Independence* were gone as well, killed off by declining passenger loads, sagging profits, and the escalating expense of simply running US-flag liners.

In that final season for the *United States*, her owners were often struggling just to find enough passengers to fill her 1,800 or so berths on those five-day crossings to Le Havre and Southampton. Her diminishing revenues could barely make a dent in the ever-soaring costs of operating such an expensive ship (she had, in fact, gone into the red in the very early 1960s, just as she reached her eighth year of service). And as if to twist the knife even further still, the American maritime unions became increasingly troublesome—increased demands, increased wages, certainly increased strikes (or at least the threat of them). The management at United States Lines had to face the obvious: the era of the *United States*, the days of the big American liner on the Atlantic (and almost everywhere else) were over. It was simply no longer profitable. Certainly, any lingering sense of prestige, of maritime glory, was not enough to please those head office accountants or Washington benefactors (almost all US flag liners were subsidized). But that boardroom decision, if it was even actually made in the Company boardroom, was kept a tight, a very tight, secret.

The *United States* sailed to Newport News as if she would return. It would be back to work as usual, in a month or so, for her 1,000 crew members. Of course, there were rumours. Some said she would return only for the winter cruises; other thought there would be at least one further Atlantic crossing; yet others, perhaps the most wildly optimistic, predicted another full season to Europe. In the end, the actual overhaul was begun—the painting, the cleaning, and the fixing were underway—when word was flashed from the Lower Broadway headquarters. Stop everything!

This is the story of the greatest American-built superliner ever, a ship of genius, the last Yankee on the North Atlantic, and, perhaps more notable still, the last in the illustrious and mighty line of Blue Riband champions. It tells of her design and creation, her triumphant maiden trips, her glory days of service, her passengers and crew, of the *America* and the United States merchant fleet in transition, and finally of the withdrawal of the supership herself—the nearly forgotten years of limbo at Norfolk, the new owners and their plans for revival, and then, more recently, the auction, the stripping down, the sad decay.

But this is also a story of a great seafarer, a man who knows and loves ships, especially the *United States*. Commodore Leroy Alexanderson's career is certainly one of the most illustrious of all—beginning in the Depression era of little freighters to the Far East, then reassignment to the luxury ships. After heroic wartime duties, Captain Alexanderson could not have realized that he would one day master not only the pride of the American fleet but the fastest merchant ship ever built. And then, from proud father of the great ship, he would become the watchful grandparent, guarding the sad and unhappy child. No one is closer to that ship than he is.

The story of the SS *United States* is a tale of a past era, of a bygone time, of happier days perhaps. Certainly, she was a symbol of her day. One of the most outstanding vessels ever built, she was also beloved of many—and remains so to this day. Much has been written about her and more needs to be written, more information and insights shared. I hope this book is a fitting continuation.

William H. Miller
Hoboken, New Jersey

Chapter 1

The Commodore and his Ships

The first snow of the autumn season had just begun to fall. Very quickly, everywhere was under a white blanket. A sort of melancholy took hold. Certainly it was the perfect mood and setting for reminiscing. Inside the rather stately and sturdy looking red-brick house, where I would spend many hours, was a cosy world of not just warmth and every comfort, but of wonderful memories—recollections of a long career at sea, of ships, many of them well known, of the personalities who worked and sailed them, of bygone and very different times. In his pleasant study, I sat across from Commodore Leroy J. Alexanderson. Herein begins the story of not just a seaman and his ship, but a great seaman and a very great ship—the last transatlantic Blue Riband champion, the superliner *United States*.

The study, which faced through a glass door onto a snowy garden that contained a grand old oak, was itself a room filled with memories. So much of it echoed the Commodore's long and brilliant career. There were miniature models of several well-known American ocean liners—the *Washington*, the *America*, and of course the *United States*. Several photos of the *Big U* were hung about. There was an impressive collection of mementoes and keepsakes and treasures: a large sterling seashell given by the deck officers of the *America*, a commendation letter from President Truman, a watch from Prince Faud (now the King) of Saudi Arabia, and an ornate gold model of a sailing ship from the Mayor of Lisbon. There were photos taken on the bridge of the *United States*, a brass clock from the officers' log room, and chairs from the Captain's dayroom. There was the inevitable retirement clock, a gift from the United States Lines, and a family present: a needlepoint of the superliner. In the nearby dining-room of the house were glass-cased collections of United States Lines china and crystal, and an aluminium flower vase. The latest addition was a gift from Richard Hadley, owner of the *United States* since 1979-80. It reminded us of what the ship might have become—an active cruiseship. A framed painting of the 'new' *United States* depicted with an added upper deck, different funnel markings, her kingposts and booms removed, rebuilt aft decks, and—rather oddly—her radar mast above the bridge missing. Surely, the latter was an oversight. In all, the Commodore's collection was impressive. All of it served as constant reminders of a seafarer and his ships.

Quite coincidentally, as we began the first of our fifteen or so hours of taped interviews, the main object of our conversations was not very far away. Only a few miles from the Commodore's home, the *United States* herself was at berth— rusted and neglected, moored in place for nearly two decades, and caught in a long saga of rumour and uncertainty. There had always been a hope that she would finally be revived, that she'd be rebuilt to something close to the depiction on the Commodore's wall, and that she'd one day sail mostly tropic seas as a restyled, rejuvenated cruiseship. Her fans—and there are legions of them—anxiously await the day when they can once again sail aboard the world's fastest ocean liner. But it seems not to be her fate. She seems never destined to leave Virginia waters, except perhaps for the scrappers. Her future seems less and less bright, her condition continuously deteriorating.

The Commodore then drove a sporty Jaguar. It bore the appropriate licence plate: BIG U 2. Together, we went over to Hampton Roads to visit the once great liner on a crisp windswept day. The golden afternoon sun highlighted the decay of the mammoth ship, casting a very real mood of sadness, loneliness, and isolation around her. We walked aboard—perhaps the 10,000th time for the Commodore. Momentarily, I could only think back to the days of sparkling splendour, of spit 'n polish, the salutes and the cheers, the high pitch of yet another gala Atlantic crossing. But on that day, the mood was very different: cold and dreary and certainly uninviting. Two elderly security guards greeted us at the small entrance on B Deck. The Commodore is still very imposing, unquestionably impressive, and still very much in charge. There were quick nods of acknowledgement followed by brief chatter. The king was returning, but to a neglected palace and not through the main gates but a side door that lacked the uniformed sentries. How it had all changed, how diminished it had all become. But despite it all, and that damp and darkened setting, the Commodore was in so many ways still the master of the *Big U*. Without even the slightest sense of confusion, he knew his way to every door and back stairwell and through the labyrinth of dimly lit and often littered corridors and alleyways. Filtered sunlight poured in through some windows and portholes, but only to reveal that the cabins had been stripped and some evidently vandalized. Barren ballrooms and empty lounges had very little that hinted of those long ago afternoon bingo games, evening concerts, and late night parties. The Windsors and the Eisenhowers and some of the Kennedys once danced here, and then there was Rita Hayworth and Greta Garbo and Grace Kelly. It was now all ten thousand midnights ago. The Commodore grew increasingly sentimental. The visit would have to be cut short. It was as if we were touring the upstairs bedrooms of an ancestral home that had long since gone to seed. Amidst the sadness, melancholy, and poignancy there was also a sense of question and frustration. Why? What a sad fate for such a great and famous ship, the engineering wonder of her time, and the most popular single ocean liner of her day. There was more than the usual silence on the way home. Understandably, the Commodore doesn't want to see the ship much anymore. The visits have become too painful.

The Commodore remained a handsome and distinguished looking man, with silvery hair, a commanding manner, and always perfectly attired. He was born on 27 June 1910, in the Bronx, New York. Both his parents were Swedish immigrants who had voyaged across the North Atlantic and settled in the New World. His father, Johannes Alexander Alexanderson, was born in Knacka, a suburb of Stockholm, and later attended agricultural college. He came to the United States in 1895, when he was 22. His mother, Freda Maria Peterson, was born in Filipstad and lived on a farm. She came to America in 1885, at the age of seven, and settled in Brooklyn, a city well known for its Scandinavian population. The Commodore's parents met in New York City in 1897 and, after their marriage, settled in Manhattan. His father was then a partner in a local gymnasium and Turkish bath, a forerunner of the present-day health and fitness centres. He taught wrestling and was himself an amateur wrestler and weight-lifter. However, when the gymnasium was sold, he turned to the wine business, first with a champagne company and then with a firm that sold altar wines.

The Alexandersons lived in the Bronx, north-east of New York City, until just after the First World War, in 1919. They then moved to Sheepshead Bay in Brooklyn, where they built their own house. There were four children, all first-generation Americans: George, born in 1903, Helen, 1907;

Leroy, 1910; and finally Howard, 1913. Their father died in 1946 and their mother in 1960. Their daughter Helen had died in 1908, when barely a year old, and brother George passed away in 1954. Howard retired from Bendix Aviation as director of engineering of their Utica division. He now resides in New Hartford, New York, and Naples, Florida with his wife Barbara.

Young Leroy had attended the public school system and graduated, in 1928, from Brooklyn's James Madison High School. He had just developed a strong fascination for far-away travel, which meant, of course, that he wanted to travel by sea. In fact, a career as a seaman seemed a very good future, and his brother George had gone on to South America as an ordinary seaman in his high school days. Later, he sailed to Europe. All of this captured the imagination of young Leroy, who applied to and was soon accepted by the New York State Maritime Academy. He took his classes aboard an old auxiliary barkentine, the USS *Newport*, which was then moored in New York harbour, off Liberty Island (then known as Bedloe's Island). She was both accommodation and classroom to students. 'We used to get there on the ferry from the Statue of Liberty that then connected to Manhattan,' he fondly recalled. A success, he was in the graduating class of June 1930.

But his maritime career might never have been.

A date with a young lady named Virginia Merritt almost scuttled my maritime career before it began. I was aboard the *Newport*, which was then in the New York Navy Yard getting ready for her annual summer cruise. I told the cadet on gangway watch: 'After taps, I'm going over the gangway.' We had been loading stores onto the ship from a boxcar on the pier that day. I went down the gangway and slipped around the end of the boxcar and ran right into Captain Tomb, the Academy's superintendent. I saluted and said, 'Good evening, sir', and dashed off. It was the worst date I ever had. I was so worried about getting caught. The next day, at Captain's Mast, they read me the riot act. I should have been dismissed from the Academy, but instead I was confined to the ship for three months. The worst part was calling my mother to tell her that I couldn't come home on leave. She said, 'It serves you right.' That episode almost ruined my career.

He had only two weeks between ships when he married Dorothea Ranken in 1934 and together they would have three children: Barbara, John, and Linda. 'It was soon after my marriage,' he said, 'that I decided to break into passenger ships in order to have a more consistent schedule and, of course, to be at home more often. I missed the birth of my first child, my daughter Barbara. My brother George took

my wife to the hospital. These were the pitfalls of a seaman's life. If you took leave, you weren't paid. I can't say enough about my dear wife Dot. She had to go it alone so often and had to be both mother as well as father to our children. The wife of a seaman was a tremendous task. They deserve all the praise in the world.

'During my first two years of my marriage, I had to remain with the Isthmian Line freighters and so continued to go on long voyages to ports all over the world: Hong Kong, Shanghai, Yokohama, Manila, Singapore, the remote Dutch East Indian islands. It was a job, which was very important in those days. I was particularly lucky because I was an officer when most of my classmates were still serving as sailors. But the real stroke of good luck was again my brother George. He had a friend at the prestigious United States Lines. He introduced me to their marine superintendent. Isthmian was very nice about it all and said that if I left, I could return in six months if it didn't work out.'

United States Lines was then part of a giant combine, the International Mercantile Marine, IMM for short. This also included the Panama Pacific Line, which had three splendid liners—the 20,000-ton *California*, *Pennsylvania*, and *Virginia*

Commodore Alexanderson is third from the left in this view dating from 1936, aboard Panama Pacific Line's *California*. (*Alexanderson Collection*)

21

Freshly refitted for her entry into South American service and restyled with a new single funnel, the former *California* became the *Uruguay* for the American Republics Line. She is shown here, in 1938, berthed in Hoboken. (*Author's Collection*)

—on intra-coastal services between New York and California via the Panama Canal. 'I was made senior third officer on the *California*. It was a lucky assignment. Of course, we didn't make much money in those days— about $125 a month. But unlike the freighters, I knew I'd have a fixed schedule. From the first trip aboard the *California*, I knew that I would be back in 35 days, the full roundtrip. We'd go from New York to Havana, Cristobal, make an early morning transit of the Canal, then load bananas at Balboa and sail up to San Pedro (Los Angeles) and then to San Francisco. Then we'd do the reverse after a couple of days in Frisco. We used to return to New York on Monday mornings and then sail on the following Friday. We used to pass our sister ships en route.'

'I thought they were successful ships—big liners with large cargo capacities. Some of the cargos were general freight out to the West Coast, bananas up to California and then fruits from the West Coast back to New York. We also carried dairy products. The *California* was 601 feet long and had two classes for passengers, first and tourist (384 first class, 363 tourist class). She was nice and well decorated, but of course wasn't air conditioned.'

This Panama Pacific trio of liners were, in fact, unsuccessful financially and were considered far too big for that intra-coastal service. They were withdrawn in 1938 and, in that era of President Franklin D. Roosevelt's Good Neighbour Policy with Latin America, they were reassigned by the US Government, which actually owned them, to the American Republics Line, a division of the well-known New York-based Moore McCormack Lines.

These three ships were laid up at New York for a time and then were considered to be a better fleet on the East Coast of South America run. The *California* returned to her builders at Newport News and was outfitted in preparation for this new venture. We were loaned to Moore McCormack to start the service, remembering that I was employed by United States Lines. I was first officer in the renamed *Uruguay*. The two original stacks had been removed and modernized with one larger stack, which actually proved to be a mistake because this had less ventilation. The ships were still owned by the Government and leased to Moore McCormack. I sailed with the *Uruguay* on her first trips to Rio de Janeiro, Santos, Montevideo, and Buenos Aires, which meant a 38-day roundtrip in and out of New York.

In June 1939, Captain Alexanderson was recalled to the United States Lines and first assigned to the combination passenger-cargo liner *President Roosevelt* and then to one of the largest American liners of her time, the *Manhattan*.

I was in the *Manhattan*, in September 1939, on the day of the Nazi attack on Poland. We were at Le Havre at the time and bound

Commodore Alexanderson is on the far right in this 1938 view, aboard the South America-bound *Uruguay*. (*Alexanderson Collection*)

SS United States

for Hamburg. But the last part of the trip was cancelled. We were carrying, in addition to passengers, a cargo of copper bars that were bound for Germany, but they were seized by the French and so never delivered. Immediately, we were given augmented accommodation. Cots were placed in the public rooms. One public room was for men, the other for women. Extra showers were installed by carpenters from shore that were hurriedly employed to do the work. We carried far more passengers than usual, taking worried tourists and anxious refugees to New York. We made several hurried sailings—few passengers going eastwards, but filled westbound. We had neutrality markings painted along the sides and so I do not recall any close calls.

That December, as the urgency of war in Europe and brewing troubles out in the Pacific heightened, Alexanderson was called to duty by the US Navy.

I was assigned to the USS *Melville,* a destroyer tender. I joined her at San Diego and we sailed out to Pearl Harbor and later were posted to the Caribbean—to Guantanamo in Cuba and to Puerto Rico. Later, we went over to Londonderry in Northern Ireland to service the Lend Lease destroyers that had been given to Britain. Afterward, we were sent to Reykjavik in Iceland and then finally to

United States Lines' *President Roosevelt* was a combination passenger-cargo liner that served on the North Atlantic between New York, Plymouth, Le Havre, and Hamburg. (*United States Lines*)

New York for an overhaul. Next, we were sent down to South America, where I remained until 1944.

Once back home, I then received orders to go out to the West Coast to take command of the USS *Livingston* at San Francisco. This ship was a Liberty ship-assault transport and, after various training exercises in the Hawaiian islands area, we took part in the invasions at Majuro, Kwajalein, Saipan, and Tinian. We took troops from the 27th Division. The *Livingston* had an all-Navy crew and could take troops, which were housed in the holds. We carried about 1,500. On our very first trip, we had delivered a full load of Seabees to Pearl Harbor.

Certainly, this wartime period created far different conditions from the Captain's comparatively tranquil voyages in those Isthmian freighters of the glamorous sailings in the likes of the *California* and *Manhattan*. 'We had a very close call at Saipan,' he recalled. 'One morning, a Japanese torpedo plane came in and then homed-in on us and finally dropped his torpedo. He nearly got caught in our mast. The torpedo went right up under the centre part of our ship. The flyer was never caught. We later took on more troops in these Pacific islands, including part of the 15th Marines, an artillery group, plus 250 Japanese prisoners of war that were being sent to Pearl Harbor. I was then relieved and told that I was to be given command of another new ship. I was detached from the *Livingston* at Eniwetok, in August 1944, and returned to the United States.'

Another assignment now awaited Alexanderson. Constant change was part of a seaman's life, and this was especially true during the hectic years of wartime.

That November, after some leave, I was given command of the USS *Gage*, an assault transport. My wife and I drove across the country, visiting the Grand Canyon, and then went to Seattle to await completion of the ship. The *Gage* was actually commissioned at Astoria, Oregon. She was a Victory-class transport capable of carrying 1,500 combat-ready troops. We sailed from Astoria on Thanksgiving morning (November 1944), a cold, bleak, rainy day.

The *Gage* later picked up a full load of troops at Oakland, California, just across from San Francisco, and we sailed— unescorted—to the South Pacific, to the Tulagi-Guadalcanal area. There we joined an amphibious transport group. At Guadalcanal, we picked up part of the 6th Marines, who were bound for Okinawa, and we were in there for the D-Day Landings. We laid offshore and ferried the troops in landing craft. We had a medical team and so we took wounded onboard. We later returned to Pearl Harbor and then to Seattle. At the end of the war in the Pacific, in August 1945, I was detached from the *Gage* and returned to the East Coast. My daughter had been born while I was on the *Gage*. I had received word, by telegram, in the Pacific. This was the special joy of coming home. She was already three months old and she was named Linda.

My son said, 'You know, Daddy, we have a new baby sister.' These were his words of greeting when I arrived at New York. Once again, I had missed the birth of one of my children. My wife had to be both mother and father. There was so little time for family.

Afterward, Captain Alexanderson had to return to the Navy Department and next was assigned to the C4-class transport *General Leroy Eltinge*, a 12,000 tonner. He had asked for another ship and this was his posting.

The *Eltinge* had a capacity of 3,200 and was being readied when I joined her for the pick-up of a full load of troops at Karachi. They had served in the Burma campaigns. We went out through the Mediterranean and Suez to Karachi and then returned to New York, to Hoboken actually. We carried 2,800 troops in the holds and another 400 officer-passengers in 4-berth cabins. The food was good on board and we took care of everyone. This was an all-male ship—no women at all. But from Hoboken, we took on three or four nurses and went out to Shanghai via Panama. We took author John Hersey as a passenger. We arrived there two or three days after Christmas 1945. We were there for about five days and berthed right up the river near the city, near the old Broadway Mansions Hotel. Ashore, I met many friends of my brother George, who was a press photographer.

It was freezing in Shanghai. The Japanese had removed all of the radiators from the hotel and so many of its occupants (mainly news reporters) would come down to the ship just to get warm. We loaded troops and some medical cases and civilians that had been interned there all during the war—nuns and priests and Red Cross workers. We also had Army flyers and WACs and a company of Marines. We then crossed to Manila and put some of our worst medical cases ashore. We were worried about our female passengers and so called them altogether in the mess and gave out a strict warning. We didn't even want them to shake hands with the men. We stressed good morals.

We sailed from Manila to Seattle, but before we offloaded the passengers there was a full inspection by local Naval authorities. One passenger stressed, 'We may not have good morale, but good morals.' The Captain ran a very strict ship!

Afterward, in early 1946, we made a roundtrip to Korea—troops over and troops back. We even took an Army Major General who would not fly. It seems that he didn't trust the maintenance of wartime planes. The General was asked to dine with me, in the master's quarters, but had to settle for a 4-berth room, the smallest on board. Ships like the *Eltinge* were very plain—designed to do a job. They were Kaiser-built ships—very basic. We were then ordered from Seattle down to San Diego to pick up a group of German prisoners-of-war, the same ones who had delivered the Nazi warship *Prinz Eugen* as a war prize to Philadelphia. We had to pick up the nucleus of officers who had moved the ship through the Panama Canal to the West Coast. She later got a US crew and went out to the atomic bomb testing site in the Pacific and was blown up. We took the Germans onboard by launches, directly from the anchored *Prinz Eugen* to the anchored *General Eltinge*. I met with the German commander, who later told me that the German Navy never wanted to go to war. It was the politicians he blamed. We took this group to New York and they were placed on Riker's Island. The *Eltinge* herself was then turned over to the Army Transport Service (later the Military Sea Transportation Service and later still Military Sealift Command) at a Brooklyn shipyard. It was June 1946. My father had just passed away and I had missed the funeral. It was very difficult—I missed so much. When my mother died years later, in 1960, I missed her funeral as well.

For his distinguished war service, Captain Alexanderson received many awards from the Navy including the American Defense Medal with Star, American Theatre Medal, Asiatic Pacific Theatre Medal with Three Stars, China Service Medal with Fleet Clasp, Victory Medal World War II, and the Naval Reserve Medal.

I rejoined United States Lines, in September 1946, and was assigned to the liner *Washington*. She had not yet been refitted and was carrying dependants home from Europe. I stayed with her for three months, until that December. We were running back and forth between New York, Southampton, and Le Havre. There were lots of war brides and military families. The ship was later restored slightly, but never again to a full luxury passenger ship.

Another well-known United States Lines passenger ship, the *Washington*, was not fully restored after Second World War trooping duties but instead ran a European austerity service with refugees, war brides, and troops. (*United States Lines*)

Her sister, the *Manhattan*, was never restored at all. That December, I was sent to the *America*, then just refitted after her war duties.

Aboard the *America*, on Voyage No 3, I was executive officer under Commodore Harry Manning, one of the greatest United States Lines' skippers. We restored the Company's transatlantic luxury services. We used to anchor and tender at Cherbourg, because the docks of Le Havre were still devastated, and then went to Southampton. I enjoyed my time in the *America*, which was then the flagship of the United States Lines.

It was during this stint, in March 1954, that Captain Alexanderson's beloved brother George died. An award-winning staff photographer for the *New York Times*, he was bound for a Scandinavian honeymoon when he died on board the Swedish liner *Stockholm*. He was buried at sea. Captain Alexanderson was only 60 miles away aboard the *America*, but travelling in the opposite direction. He had been notified by radio telegram.

Following the *America*, the Captain was transferred, at least for a short time, to the United States Lines' freight division.

In 1950, I was posted to the *American Forwarder*, a C2-class freighter of 8,200 tons. I would be her master, replacing Captain Stanley Thompson. I stayed with her for three years, until 1953, when I returned to the *America* as executive officer and relieving master. The *American Forwarder* plied the North Atlantic, between New York, Philadelphia, Baltimore, Norfolk, and then back to New York before sailing over to Liverpool and then through the Manchester Ship Canal to Manchester. We then went up to Glasgow to load whisky and then over to Dublin and then to Boston and finally back to New York. Sometimes we'd change and go from Liverpool to Dublin and then up to Glasgow. We used to pick up horses in Dublin. We'd fit stalls in hatch 5—portable stalls, of course. We'd even carry a special horse handler. We had a crew of about fifty and had space for about a dozen passengers. She was a good little ship, built at Wilmington in North Carolina by a wartime subsidiary of the big Newport News Shipbuilding & Dry Dock Company. Of course, in those days, aboard ships like the *American Forwarder*, we often had three or four days in port. Everything was determined by cargo, the loading and unloading, and the schedules were often determined just hours before. United States Lines had about fifty-five ships in those days. The freight office was located right on the Chelsea Docks in Manhattan.

Captain Alexanderson, after a two-year stint aboard the *America* (1953-5), received word, in July 1955, that he was being 'loaned' to Newport News Shipbuilding to assist with the trials of the new supercarrier *Forrestal*. 'I was being paid by the shipyard at the time and several other United States Lines' officers came as well—Dick Ridington, Bob Brooks, Dirk Meyers, and John Tucker. We stayed at Newport News

from the end of July to the end of September to complete the trials which had been delayed several times by bad weather.'

This event was duly recorded in the July-August 1955 edition of the *Shipyard Bulletin*, the Newport News journal:

At exactly 3:00 pm on August 29th, the world's largest and mightiest naval vessel, the *Forrestal*, came to life and moved slowly from a Yard pier. This was the culmination of almost three years of labor by thousands of workers at Newport News and other thousands all over the United States. What had started as a few lifeless steel plates on July 14th 1952, had been shaped into a ship that, to her builders, was an object of beauty. Every workman, no matter how small his contribution, was proud of the part he had played in bringing this mighty vessel to life.

Originally, two trials had been scheduled for the *Forrestal*. A Builder's Trial from 4:00 am Tuesday, August 16th, to 7:00 pm Wednesday, August 17th; and a Preliminary Acceptance Trial from August 29th to September 2nd. Hurricane Diane, however, had different ideas about the first scheduled sea trials and caused their cancellation. Later, thousands of persons watched from the Shipyard and waterfront of Newport News as the *Forrestal* was maneuvered from her outfitting berth into the James River. As soon as the port bow had cleared the pier, tugs were waiting to aid the ship's propellers in pushing the bow around to head the giant ship seaward. Those of the 2,300 persons on board not busy operating the ship were watching the shore and the dozens of small boats accompanying the *Forrestal* and kept a safe distance by the Coast Guard. Because of the ship's size there was no problem in finding a vantage point from which to watch.

As the *Forrestal* majestically rode past the Chesapeake & Ohio Railway piers on the Newport News waterfront, the tide pointed

Captain Alexanderson served aboard the freighter *American Forwarder* from 1950 until 1953. She was then one of some 55 vessels in the United States Lines fleet. One of her near-sisters, the *American Leader*, is shown here, in December 1947, as seen from the liner *America*. (*Alexanderson Collection*)

the bows of 35 merchant ships in the harbor toward the carrier in a seeming silent salute. A Navy blimp and a helicopter cruised overhead. At 3:54 pm, while the *Forrestal* was off Stuart Gardens, the ship's speaker advised: 'Dismiss all tugs and thank you very much.'

The trials were a huge success and the *Forrestal* was soon accepted into the Navy's active fleet. Afterward, Captain Alexanderson was posted to the superliner *United States*. The official transfer came on 27 September 1955, when the world's fastest merchant ship was just over two years old. 'I was quite surprised. Earlier, when I went to the *America* as executive officer and relieving master to Captain Milde, I said that "That will be the day when the marine superintendent gives me command of that ship." I was very surprised. On that first trip on the *America*, we had fog in the Hudson River. It was just four in the afternoon. We had to go down very slowly. You had to mind your ps and qs—the river was very crowded with barges and carfloats and tugs and ferries. It was quite a beginning. When I went over to the *United States*, it was quite a feather in my cap.' But not everyone preferred the big liners, not even the world's fastest liner and newest transatlantic super queen.

At the time of her completion in the summer of 1955, the supercarrier *Forrestal* ranked as the world's largest and mightiest naval vessel. Captain Alexanderson assisted with her sea trials. (*Alexanderson Collection*)

Some Company people preferred the liners and others preferred the freighters. I had been in the passenger ships and so preferred them. There were fast turnarounds and a more exact schedule and, of course, you were home more often. The liners had fixed schedules. It wasn't always easy, however. Occasionally, we'd run late. If we didn't make it at 8 in the morning, they'd hold us off until 1 in the afternoon or then until 3. But if we couldn't make 3, they'd

hold us until 7 in the evening or so just to avoid the so-called 'golden hour' between 5 and 7 when the stevedores got double-time. Once in a while, sometimes in winter, we'd have delays, but it didn't happen too often. The *United States* was a very punctual ship. On board the *United States*, I especially enjoyed being with Commodore John Anderson. The first time I had met him was out in the Philippines. He was then aboard one of the American Pioneer Line freighters. It was pre-war, in 1931, and I was with Isthmian at the time. He was already a skipper. He was a very fine gentleman. He ran a good ship. I also enjoyed sailing with his predecessor, Commodore Manning.

In November 1959, Captain Alexanderson was notified that he had been selected for promotion to the rank of Rear Admiral in the US Naval Reserve. He was now Rear Admiral Alexanderson—one of the very few naval reservists in the merchant marine to rise above the rank of captain. Years later, at the time of his retirement in 1976, he rated as the only Naval Reserve officer of flag rank within the United States Merchant Marine.

In 1980, at the New York State Maritime Acadamy's alumni banquet and the 50th anniversary of his own graduation from that institution, the Captain delivered the after-dinner speech. Master of the *United States*, the pride of the American fleet, he was aptly selected to be the guest of honour that evening. His speech began: 'When I was first asked to be guest of honour at this dinner, my first thought was that the committee had reviewed the list of graduates of the class of 1930 and had chosen my name because it began with the letter "A" and was at the top of the list. My next thought was what I was going to speak about at a dinner like this and I have worried about it for months because I am not as much a home at the speaker's table as I am on the bridge of a ship.'

Captain Alexanderson outlined his already extensive career, mentioning the ships and shipowners that he had served. In closing, he spoke of the mighty *United States* and of the state of the merchant marine: 'About the SS *United States*, as you all know, she took the Blue Riband of the North Atlantic on her maiden voyage, averaging 35.59 knots on her eastbound passage and 34.51 knots on the westbound cross ing, the first time any ship has broken both eastbound and westbound records during the same voyage. When the ship first started running, she was scheduled for twenty-two roundtrips a year, to Le Havre and Southampton, and five voyages terminating at Bremerhaven. Gradually, this has been increased and we are now scheduled for twenty-four round voyages and ten calls to Germany. To date, we have steamed 1,243,000 miles, a feat no other ship accomplished in a like period of time. We have carried over 525,000 passengers and are extremely proud of our ability to maintain schedule, our reputation for service to passengers, and our superb cuisine. Our deck and engineering officers are almost all graduates of one of the various maritime academies.'

He then continued on the subject of general US-flag shipping:

With regard to the American Merchant Marine, it is true that ship-building went into a slump after World War Two, but now that various steamship companies have commenced their replacement programmes, it is hoped that the future of the Merchant Marine will be brighter.

This will offer a new opportunity to graduates of the various maritime academies who have chosen the sea as their profession. The new ships building and planned will offer broader horizons for the development of the graduates' abilities, keeping in mind that the American Merchant Marine is and always will be the life-line of our country, and is the means of supply of our armed forces located throughout the world.

However, there is one problem today that faces most steamship companies. This is, the choosing and employment of the younger officers. Years ago, an officer was directly employed by the steam-ship company. Today, this system is no longer possible and some-thing should be done to correct this situation. I do know that in the past year and half with the United States Lines Company, we have not given employment on a permanent basis to any new officers. This is a grave source of worry both to management and to all who are in command.

It is our hope that in future labour negotiations, some provisions will be made to provide opportunities for the recent gradu-ates of the maritime academies. After all, our Government has spent large sums of money to provide the maritime industry with well trained and qualified young officers.

Returning to the *United States* on her regular runs on the Atlantic, Captain Alexanderson relieved Commodore Ander-son forty-four different times before he himself became Com-modore. 'We had several captains—John Tucker, Dick Ridington and, on several occasions, Dick Patterson. The *United States* had some very fine masters. We weren't mak-ing the big salaries in those days. Commodore Anderson made about $23,000 a year at the time. The big salaries came after the *United States* was laid up. Today's containership cap-tains easily make $100,000 a year. When I left in 1976, I made about $45,000 a year as Commodore of the United States Lines.'

One of Captain Alexanderson's duties when in command

of the *Big U* was to take the daily 'phone calls from the man most associated with the ship, William Francis Gibbs, her creator.

Mr Gibbs was in a word a perfectionist. He expected you to do the best. He would help you in return and in every way. If you needed something, he would often go personally to the United States Lines offices to get it. He'd put his two cents in. Oddly, however, he made only one voyage in the ship, the maiden voyage. But from that time on, he never once sailed with us. Even on the overhaul trips, between New York and Virginia, he refused. Instead, his car would take him to Pennsylvania Station and he'd take the train down to either Richmond or Washington. A car would meet him and take him over to the shipyards. He'd do the same in reverse. But Mrs Gibbs used to travel with us once a year and also made a number of cruises.

Mr Gibbs called every day to the ship. Sometimes this was difficult. Sometimes you'd be up all night because of fog and then you'd just get to bed when the Radio Room would call and say we have Mr Gibbs on the 'phone. Sometimes he'd just say, 'How's the weather?' He'd then talk to the Chief Engineer. And he'd always meet you, no matter what time.

William Francis Gibbs evidently never quite looked the part, however. According to Captain Alexanderson:

He looked almost down and out. He used to have his shoes and his hat constantly remade. When he was here in Newport News, he used to attend St John's Episcopal Church and place a $50 bill in the collection plate. I remember once when we were late—we docked at 7 in the evening. He came aboard in his opera clothes, full white tie and tails. He said he thought it was more important to come down here to the ship than to the opening of the opera.

Toward the end, someone else from his office would call the ship. We didn't hear from Mr Gibbs. We'd ask, of course, 'How is Mr Gibbs?' They'd say, 'He's at an important meeting.' Actually, he was in the hospital—but he would not allow this to be admitted. He died while I was on board, in September 1967, and when we sailed past that day, we dipped the ensign and blew the whistle. Actually, it was something we always did. He'd be watching from his office at 21 West Street in Lower Manhattan. Of course, we couldn't go to his funeral.

We were also offering that same salute to Dick West, the chairman of the Board of the Irving Trust Company. He'd be fifty stories above Wall Street in his executive dining room. Somebody there used to hang out a huge white tablecloth as we saluted with three blasts. Mr West was a frequent passenger and a good friend to all of us. But once, we failed to blow the whistle and we quickly received a radio message asking why we forgot.

Once, when I was on leave, my wife and I were invited to that tower restaurant and together we all watched as the *United States* sailed past. Mr West thought of the ship as his yacht. On another time, just before sailing, he had come up to my quarters for a drink when I received a message asking if Aristotle Onassis, the millionaire Greek shipping tycoon, could come up. To my surprise, he and Dick West were old friends. My steward Pete was a Greek, and he and Mr Onassis quickly began to speak their native language. Onassis was very friendly. I, of course, drank my usual: iced tea. It just looked like the Canadian Club Whisky that Dick West preferred.

Captain Alexanderson had at least three names aboard the *Big U*. 'I was Captain or Commodore, of course, I was also Alex. And I was Ajax. And, of course, and like all skippers, I was the Old Man. Sometimes, I was even Captain Ajax. I was Ajax because I was supposed to be so clean, Ajax being the well known household cleanser. Other officers reported that his white-glove inspections were especially demanding.

'The *Big U* was spotless to the very end', reported the Captain proudly. 'I'd even check for smells. I have a very sensitive nose. We had the occasional cockroach once in a while, in damp areas and when we loaded stores in cardboard boxes, but we'd get rid of them quickly. We had to pass very strict health inspections. I could never stand a roach and never ever saw a rat on board. I remember also that there was at least one cat aboard the older liners. In fact, I remember several cats and their kittens aboard the old *Manhattan*. They used to come aboard from the New York piers. But there were no cats on the *Big U.*'

There was an 'old sea dog' aboard the superliner, however. This was Chota Peg, certainly the most travelled dog in all of the American fleet. He logged 2,000,000 nautical miles in fourteen years aboard passenger ships. The 14½-year-old cocker spaniel finally died aboard the *United States* on 1 July 1957. Pete, the Captain's steward, discovered Chota Peg dead in the master's stateroom while the liner was at sea. The favoured pet was then given a sailor's funeral. His obituary appeared in both the *New York Times* and the New York *Herald Tribune*.

Chota Peg—which is Hindustani for small drink— had been the beloved pet of Commodore John Anderson. The animal had sailed with him aboard four different liners— the troopship *John Ericsson,* the *Washington,* the *America,* and finally the *United States*—since 1943. Actually, the dog had been instrumental in introducing the Commodore to his future wife, then a member of the Women's Army Corps travelling in the *Ericsson*. The dog had been bought in a Manhattan pet shop, but then lived most of its life on board ship. After his death, a United States Lines spokesman com-

mented, 'Chota Peg had been weaned aboard ship and had
gotten so used to shipboard life that he had not been ashore
for six years since 1951.'

Captain Alexanderson fondly recalled the pet:

I would care for the dog when I relieved Commodore Anderson
aboard the *United States*. It seems that his wife did not like the
dog because she felt their son was allergic to it. So the dog stayed
on the ship all the time. He stayed in our quarters and was walked
on deck. When we had guests, he was put in the bedroom with
the door closed. But once, when we were westbound on the *United
States*, Commodore Anderson called me to his office, He said 'I
just received a call from the Chief Purser that an Ambassador is
coming up to see me about keeping his dog in his cabin. Take
Chota Peg and put him in your cabin.' When the Ambassador
came in, he insisted that his dog was very clean and well behaved,
but the Commodore insisted that it was Company policy that all
dogs be kept in the ship's kennel. Just then, my steward opened

The beloved Chota
Peg, with Commodore
John Anderson aboard
the superliner *United
States*, was said to
have logged some two
million nautical miles.
(*Alexanderson Collection*)

the door to my cabin and Chota Peg ran over to where we were talking. The Commodore calmly said 'I'm a crew member—that policy doesn't apply to me!'

Pete, my steward, used to hand feed him—it seems he wouldn't eat out of a bowl. When we took him ashore at Bremerhaven or Le Havre, he would not use the steps. He was used to the elevator only. He was dearly loved. When he finally died, he was wrapped in canvas and buried at sea.

When John Anderson retired as Commodore in February 1964, Captain Alexanderson was selected as his successor. The official decree came on the 14th of that same month and, on 29 July 1966, it was authorized by General John M. Franklin, the Chairman of the Board of Directors of the United States Lines. Captain Alexanderson was appointed Commodore of the United States Lines fleet and the formal citation read:

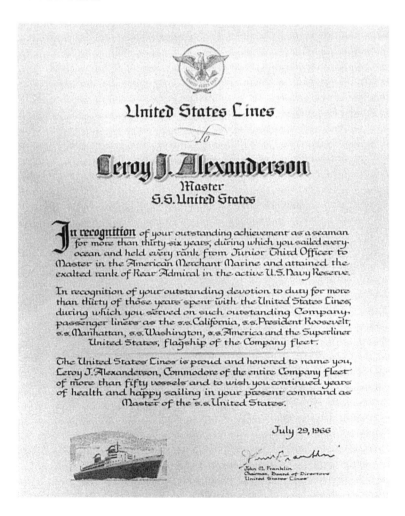

United States Lines

to

Leroy J. Alexanderson
Master
S.S. United States

In recognition of your outstanding achievement as a seaman for more than thirty-six years, during which you sailed every ocean and held every rank from Junior Third Officer to Master in the American Merchant Marine and attained the exalted rank of Rear Admiral in the active U.S. Navy Reserve.

In recognition of your outstanding devotion to duty for more than thirty of those years spent with the United States Lines, during which you served on such outstanding Company passenger liners as the s.s. California, s.s. President Roosevelt, s.s. Manhattan, s.s. Washington, s.s. America and the Superliner United States, flagship of the Company fleet.

The United States Lines is proud and honored to name you, Leroy J. Alexanderson, Commodore of the entire Company fleet of more than fifty vessels and to wish you continued years of health and happy sailing in your present command as Master of the s.s. United States.

July 29, 1966

John M. Franklin
Chairman, Board of Directors
United States Lines

The Commodore's flag was also presented to Captain, now Commodore, Alexanderson in that summer of 1966. A special ceremony was held and it was later noted in the United States Lines' newsletter: 'In a colorful ceremony on the bridge of the superliner *United States* at Pier 86 in New York, Mr William B. Rand, president of the United States Lines, presented the 56-year-old Alexanderson with the Company's Commodore's Flag—a blue eagle superimposed on a large white field with a deep red border signifying the highest rank in the Company fleet. While virtually the entire officer complement of the SS *United States* and a large contingent of unlicensed deck, engine and stewards' departments crewmen looked on, the silken ensign was run up the halyard to the ship's radar mast. The Commodore's flag will always be flown when the superliner enters or leaves port and while he is aboard the vessel at the pier.'

After the *Big U* was laid up in 1969, and after staying with her through her final decommissioning into the following spring, the Commodore was posted to a containership, the 18,700-ton *American Legion*. 'We ran the North European service—to Rotterdam, Bremerhaven, and Southampton. I made several crossings. On one of these trips, when we were two days out of the English Channel, we encountered a very bad following sea. I was told that we had some loose containers aft. They were moving side to side. We attempted to secure them, but then the ship rolled. We lost eleven containers, and one of them was hanging off the side. They'd been stacked improperly—they were too high. Two of the containers, empty tanks for carrying whisky, later floated ashore in Ireland. Another United States Lines' containership just ahead of us lost thirteen containers in the same weather.'

Both Commodore Alexanderson and the *American Legion* were later reassigned to the more extensive Far East service, from the US East Coast through the Panama Canal and then via Long Beach, Oakland, and Honolulu to the Orient—to Hong Kong, Osaka, and Yokohama—and then back to the West and finally the East Coasts. It was all reminiscent of his days with the Isthmian Line forty years before. But business for all shipping, especially expensive US-flag shipping, was becoming increasingly costly and therefore less and less economical. In fact, the American fleet was slipping deeper and deeper into troubled times and was beginning its sad decline.

The Commodore retired in 1976. This too was aptly noted in the United States Lines newsletter: 'Edward J. Heine, Jr., the Company president, announced the recent retirement from active duty of Commodore Leroy J. Alexanderson. During a lifetime career of 46 years at sea, the Commodore served as master of the famous superliner *United States* from 1964 until the lay-up of the vessel in 1969. He was appointed Commodore of the United States Lines in 1966. His most recent command was the container liner *American Legion.'*. The *New York Times*, in its 17 October 1976 edition, noted the passing as well. 'Commodores in the American Merchant Marine, especially with the disappearance of US-flag passenger ships on the East Coast, are getting scarcer than pearls in an oyster. And one of them, Captain Leroy J. Alexanderson of United States Lines, has just "swallowed the anchor", thus leaving Captain Russell McDow of Farrell Lines the distinction of being the only active merchant mariner of flag rank in this area. As for Captain Alexanderson, the one star that went with being a Commodore isn't the only one he can wear. He is also a retired Rear (two star) Admiral in the US Naval Reserve.

'Captain Alexanderson, who is 66 years old and lives in Garden City, Long Island, had mixed feelings the other day about being permanently ashore after having spent 46 years at sea. "There is enough to keep me busy, but altogether it's sort of new, and it will take a bit of time to get adjusted to being a landlubber," he said.

'Alexanderson was in command of the superliner *United States* on her last transatlantic crossing before the world's fastest passenger liner was taken out of commission in November 1969. Since then, he has been in command of cargo ships, the latest being the *American Legion*. Asked to compare being a luxury liner skipper with serving as master of a cargo ship, he said: "It's a question of dimensions. On the *Big U*, I was responsible for close to 3,000 people, 2,000 passengers and 1,000 crew; and the job called for considerable social contact with passengers. On a freighter, you would only have a crew of 40 to worry about and you have a lot more time to yourself, to unwind and to read"'.

Commodore Alexanderson moved to Hampton, Virginia after the death of his first wife Dorothea, in August 1979, and married Elizabeth Dougherty. Elizabeth and Bill Dougherty were close friends of the Alexandersons for over thirty years. Between them, they have five children, nine grandchildren, and one great-grandchild.

Although now a lonely ship, the Commodore's beloved *Big U* is practically in his own backyard. His expertise with and knowledge of the great liner remains unmatched and so, after the sale of the idle liner to United States Cruises in 1979-80, it was quite logical that he should be hired as

Commodore Alexanderson had completed 46 years at sea when he retired from the containership *American Legion* in 1976. (*Alexanderson Collection*)

a consultant to this new venture. He was naturally excited about the revival of his favourite ship and remarked at one United States Cruises' press conference: 'The main reason cruise vacations are becoming so popular is that when people go aboard a ship they can relax completely with other people waiting on them left and right. After the renovation and modernization, the *United States* is really going to be something.'

There were, of course, many, many sentimental occasions as well. He often gave interviews about the life and times of the world's fastest ocean liner. Sometimes he even led tours aboard her, often guided by little more than his perfect memory and a flashlight. One lengthy feature in the *Newport News Daily Press*, in November 1981, was appropriately titled: 'SS *United States*: A Lady in Waiting.' Part of the story read: 'The Commodore was joined on this particular

39

occasion by Dr John E. Sheedy, the chief surgeon of the liner. His career encompassed the entire seventeen-year active life of the ship. He was aboard Voyage No 1 and stayed through Voyage No 400—from the first record-breaking crossing in 1952 to the final trip from Le Havre when, on November 7th 1969, Alexanderson rang up "Finished with Engines" in New York harbor.'

Author Alexander C. Brown gave a wonderfully evocative account of the silent liner after his visit. In part of his story, he wrote:

We are now on the way up to the bridge, but Alexanderson steered us past one well-appointed three-room suite, the customary ship-board residence, he told us, of the Duke and Duchess of Windsor while making their frequent transatlantic journeys. In ocean liners, their proclaimed preference was for the *United States* over the staid, luxurious British *Queens*, a sentiment not unappreciated by the United States Lines management. The Duke and his lady generally took all meals in their suite, Alexanderson said, but at least once during a voyage, they would make a grand entrée into the first class saloon.

One more deck up put us in officers' country above the passengers. We were pointed out Chief Engineer Bill Kolbe's quarters with nearby elevator which could whisk him down to the engine room. Underneath the bridge on the port side were the cabins and offices reserved for the ship's executive officer, while on the opposite side, forward, was the Commodore's suite. Here Alexanderson sank into one of his over-stuffed chairs and, for a moment, reverted to being not only polished host to the wealthy and influential, but a true mariner in whose hands lay the direction and safety of the most magnificent nautical creation ever produced in this country, or the world for that matter.

Alexanderson told us of some of what it was like to be in command of a priceless ship on the unpredictable, never relenting North Atlantic, a malignant, restless, untrustworthy being which ever demands respect and deference.

I asked him if now, retired from going to sea, if he had kept any of his uniforms. He said that he had given away his bridge great coat, so heavy that he felt it was pulling him down into his shoes, but which was more than warm when he had been on the bridge for hours on end and while the ship was fighting a winter gale.

Too soon, it seemed, it was time to retrace our way down the labyrinth of companionways and passages which had ultimately brought us up to the ship's pilot house. Here, from a high stool near the helmsman, was the ship's command post reserved for the 'old man'. In it, Alexanderson and his predecessors had been lords of all they surveyed.

While the *United States* remained idle, even her former owners foundered. The United States Lines declared bankruptcy in November 1986 and closed its doors forever. The company that had once run the world's fastest ocean liner, as well as many other great liners and as many as fifty-five ships at one time, was suffocated in a financial storm. The Commodore and his fellow officers and crew were saddened yet further. 'The United States Lines was killed in the end,' according to Commodore Alexanderson, 'by building twelve monster containerships which were too slow. They could only do a maximum of 18 knots. They didn't have enough speed to compete with the likes of the Evergreen Line of Taiwan. There was also reduced freight rates by foreign companies and their around-the-world services. The likes of Evergreen went in both directions whereas United States Lines went eastbound only. There was also a new management at United States Lines that did not know that much about the shipping business.

'The overall company costs had become too high against the amount of cargo they took. The final blow seems to have been the rise in fuel oil prices. These diesel-driven big containerships became totally uneconomic. It is very sad that many American trained seamen are now working for foreign-flag companies. It's all a great, great shame.'

Another snowfall had hit eastern Virginia, although this was far lighter and often mixed with rain, later in the week of my first visit with the Commodore, in November 1987. On this day, we drove over to the mighty Newport News Shipyards. The weather once more created a mood of melancholy. The yard—the biggest employer in the State of Virginia—is a vast complex of offices and sheds, warehouses and cranes. A hum filled the afternoon air. But the bulk of the business now—and the reason for Newport News' survival in an era of steadily declining US shipyard operations is military—top-secret, big-budget military. It was as a guest of Rear Admiral Alexanderson that we gained our prized entry. There were, of course, the inevitable security checks. Two multi-billion dollar supercarriers were under construction and nearly 5,000 workers were employed directly on these projects. Submarine work was being carried out elsewhere in the plant.

We passed through the entrance lobby in one of the main administrative buildings and noted a pair of ornately carved pilasters saved from the mantel in the first class smoking room of the old liner *Leviathan*. Her conversion, from the captured German *Vaterland*, was a predecessor project to the building of the *United States* at this yard. Later, we were taken round by car, guided by no less than a senior vice-president, through a facility so enormous that it even has its own railway system. We passed the last pair of traditional slipways, where the cruiseships *Santa Rosa* and *Santa Paula* had been built in the late 1950s. They were the last newly-built passenger liners to come out of Newport News. The nearby building site of the *America*, launched fifty years before, was gone and had given way to a huge modular outfitting unit. Our guide also pointed out the vast building where steel had been fabricated for the *United States*. We later paused at Graving Dock 10, the birthplace of the *Big U*. Locally, the story of the liner then seemed somehow more complete: her birthplace, her final master, and the ship herself a short distance away at a Norfolk pier.

The late autumn sun began to fade. Floodlights were being switched on. A muscular Krupps-made crane was shuttling along its tracks and work crews were busy on a 900-ton section destined for the supercarrier *George Washington*. Small trucks squirrelled about almost everywhere. A train clattered past. The busy shipyard was at work, the night shifts already in place. It is now time to begin the story of the *United States*, greatest of the American liners, the last Blue Riband champion, and the ship so beloved of Commodore Leroy J. Alexanderson.

Chapter 2

America the Beautiful

'When I was first assigned to the liner *America*,' recalled Commodore Leroy Alexanderson, 'I was told never to proposition a girl on the Main Lounge dance floor because conversation tended to echo all around the room.' This was in late 1946, on Voyage No 3. It was one of the idiosyncrasies of what was then not only the flagship of the United States Lines, but the entire United States Merchant Marine as well. She had just been refitted and restored after rather hectic war duties. She was something of a dream-boat, a ship loved and admired and one that gathered a long and loyal following. To many—and the praises would continue to the very end of her days under the US flag—the *America* was considered one of the most beautiful of all American passenger ships. To some, she was the most beautiful—she was *America*, the beautiful! She was also the forerunner to the brilliant *United States*.

The 33,961-ton *America*, a moderate in size compared to some of her British, French, German, and Italian superliner rivals, was a ship of the 1930s, but she was nevertheless amongst the most modern and sophisticated. William Francis Gibbs had incorporated a host of advanced elements in her design. Conservative as she was in both size and speed (she was no Blue Riband contender), she was surely a prelude to the superliner that Mr Gibbs envisioned might be built as early as the early 1940s. The 723 ft long *America* was the test case, the pilot, and the eventual running-mate for what was still the 'drawing-board supership'. For these reasons, she deserves special attention, a chapter of her own.

The United States Lines passenger services had been hard hit by the bitter Depression years of the early 1930s. The Company had just added a pair of liners, again moderately sized, to its fleet. They were the 29,000-ton *Washington* and *Manhattan*. At the time, they were considered ideal and safe

An historic day and the beginning of the rebirth of the US fleet: Mrs Eleanor Roosevelt, wife of the American president, names the liner *America*. The date is 31 August 1939. (*Alexanderson Collection*)

Opposite The pristine hull of the brand new *America*, then the largest liner yet built in a US yard. (*Alexanderson Collection*)

investments for what was then a struggling North Atlantic trade. The Company also ran combination passenger-cargo ships in service. But the biggest complication, at least by 1934, surrounded the giant *Leviathan*, a 59,900-tonner that had been operated by the United States Lines since 1923, but without any great success. Ranking as the second largest liner afloat, the *Leviathan*'s career had been complicated by a number of afflictions: the lack of a suitable running mate to enable a balanced weekly service to be run; the strict laws of American Prohibition (which kept US-flag liners dry); the comparatively expensive American shipboard labour; and even problems with her management (there were those at United States Lines and within the government, her sponsors, who believed that she would never succeed). By the early 1930s the 950 ft long *Leviathan* was deeply in the red. She began to skip sailings and later sat out the barren winter months at her New York berth. In 1932, she was laid up. Two years later, she was reactivated, but for only four crossings. Her fate was sealed.

Her withdrawal was conditional, however. The US government made a provision for a replacement liner, one much more moderate in scale that would be a far safer investment. She would be a companion to the aforementioned team of *Washington* and *Manhattan*. Prevailing feelings were, however, that the new ship should not duplicate *Washington* and *Man-*

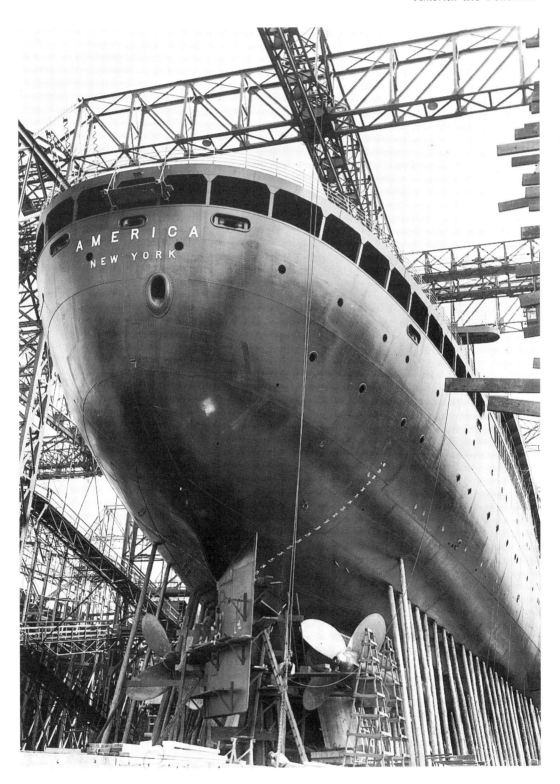

Maiden arrival at New York, in August 1940, for the brand new *America*. (*Alexanderson Collection*)

hattan but should be slightly larger, faster, improved, and certainly more distinctive. Furthermore, within the ranks of the government, there were some very serious concerns about the state of the national merchant marine. Although the US fleet in the mid 1930s was second only to that of Great Britain, with over 3,000 ships totalling 12,000,000 gross tons, these ships were generally ageing, mostly of post-First World War construction, and were perhaps less than ideal for possible emergency war use—and by 1935 the possibilities of another war, even a vast international conflict, were already looming.

The Merchant Marine Act of 1936 was subsequently enacted and, in October of that same year, the formal US Maritime Commission was formed. Its purpose: to develop and strengthen the national fleet. Plans and then building contracts were in hand almost immediately. Obviously, some projects were considered more urgent than others and a new liner for the North Atlantic was top priority. But while she would carry the national colours and reinforce the American position in the transatlantic trade, it would be her emergency potential as a large troop transport that guaranteed her creation. In fact, she was selected to be the very first ship of a new US fleet.

Designs were drawn by Gibbs & Cox, bids were submitted, and finally the order was signed. Announcements went out in October 1937. The job went to a very experienced builder, the Newport News Shipbuilding & Dry Dock Company of Virginia. She would be Hull No 1 of the Maritime

Commission's new fleet (in fact, at Newport News, she was their Yard No 369). The keel was ceremoniously laid on 22 August 1938. The choice of name seemed most appropriate: *America*.

L.A. Sawyer and W.H. Mitchell in their excellent series *From* America *to* United States, *Part I*, wrote of this new liner: 'Fitted with the most modern safety devices, her decking was laid over steel, stateroom bulkheads were of asbestos compound, furniture of steel or aluminium and upholstery fireproof. Watertight subdivision was such that should three adjacent watertight compartments become flooded, the vessel would not submerge beyond a line three inches below and parallel to the highest continuous watertight deck. Fourteen lifeboats and two rescue boats were fitted.'

With her construction deemed a priority, she was ready for launching within twelve months. The official date was set for the last day of August in that tense summer of 1939. Appropriately, Mrs Eleanor Roosevelt—the wife of the President of the United States and an increasingly popular figure in her own right—would do the honours. Over 30,000 attended the ceremony, with the new liner poetically glistening in the summer sunshine. But, on the following day, there was far more explosive news, and a shock was felt around the world: Hitler's forces invaded innocent Poland. Suddenly, the world was at war—and the entire picture changed.

A post-war cruise to the Caribbean: the *America* at Havana, in February 1950. (*Alexanderson Collection*)

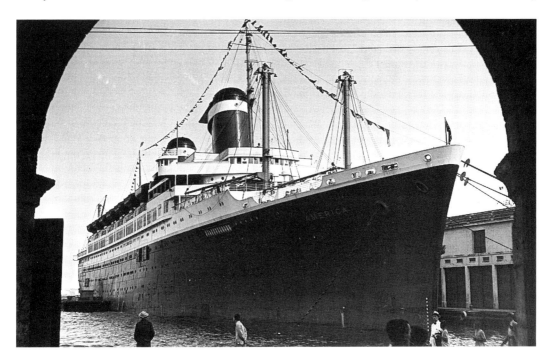

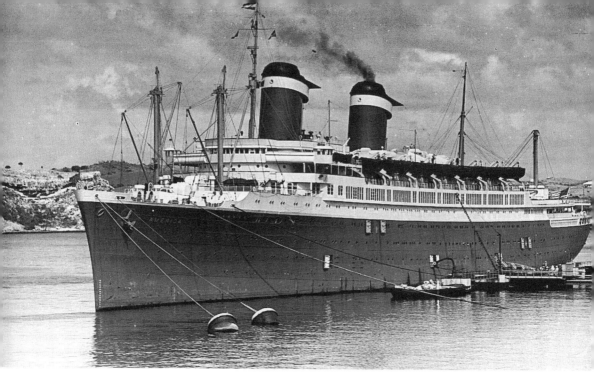

Those worries of the mid 1930s had been tragically justified.

Work on the *America* continued, perhaps even more urgently, though the gala plans for a European maiden voyage in the summer of 1940 looked less and less likely. Undoubtedly, some of the intended sparkle, the glow over the new ship, had been tarnished. The idea of a 'peacetime luxury ship' would be temporary at best. Inevitably, the transatlantic schedule was cancelled (in fact it was to be delayed for over six years); instead, thereby avoiding the possibility of a lay-up, she was sent on cruises: Bermuda, the Caribbean, even through the Panama Canal to California and back. She left on her first trip, her commercial maiden voyage, on 10 August 1940. She had had successful trials, satisfying both her builders and her owners in nearly every way (the one notable exception was that her initially squat funnels had to be heightened almost immediately because of smoke and soot problems on the aft open decks). Perhaps most importantly of all, she won high praises from the general public (gathered mostly from well-attended tours and receptions given during her maiden call at New York). The cruises were, as expected, only a temporary alternative. By the spring of 1941, she was called to duty.

The 1,046-passenger *America* was fitted out as a troop transport, with official berthing for 8,175 troops in all. She would, on occasion, exceed this total. Painted over in drab greys, she was now less recognizable, her whereabouts secret. Her war service began in June 1941. Just prior to her first trip, however, and for obvious security reasons, she was renamed

West Point. Little more than a year later, on 28 September 1942, she was transferred outright to the Navy. In all, during the war years, she would carry 300,000 troops and other military passengers. Her voyages, which were officially documented from January 1942, took her to ports all over the world: Melbourne, Bombay, Rio de Janeiro, San Francisco, Aden, Casablanca, Honolulu, Marseilles, Manila, and such lesser-known spots as Milne Bay and Massawa. She left Boston on her final troop voyage in December 1945, sailing out to Pearl Harbor and then Manila before returning to New York. Her record was both heroic and impressive, making her one of the best American troopers of those war years. She was released from active military duties in February 1946 and then transferred from the War Department back to United States Lines. Returning to her builders' yard in Virginia, she once again became the *America*.

In early November 1946, the *America* steamed triumphantly into New York harbour—still the largest liner under the US flag and in pristine condition: her funnels shimmering in red, white, and blue; her decks and upperworks in sparkling white, and her hull in traditional black (it would be made dark grey for an experimental period in the late 1940s, but when this proved impractical it reverted to black). On 14 November, booked to capacity, she set off—after a six-year delay—on her first commercial trip to Europe. This post-

Another view taken at Willemstad, Curacao, also in the winter of 1950. (*Alexanderson Collection*)

SS United States

war maiden voyage took her to Cobh and Le Havre, with turnaround at Southampton.

Her intended pre-war running-mates, the *Washington* and *Manhattan*, had also given yeoman service during the war years. However, while they were still less than fifteen years old, both ships had endured strenuous service and were well worn. The *Manhattan*, which had served as the troop carrier *Wakefield*, suffered even more serious problems, having been badly damaged by fire while at sea in September 1942. She was towed into port and, though initially thought to be beyond practical repair, underwent—no doubt to the pressing need for wartime troopers—extensive rebuilding, even losing an entire deck in the process. When she finished her trooping duties in 1946, there was little thought of reviving her for further commercial service. She remained in government hands and went almost directly to the 'mothball fleet' of idle ships, then numbering several hundred, at Jones Point, New York, in the upper Hudson River. She would not move from her moorings for nearly twenty years until, in 1965, when officially declared surplus and of no further value should another war erupt, she was sold to local scrappers at Kearny, New Jersey. When she was towed down river she passed her old berth for United States Lines at West 21st Street.

The *Washington*, renamed *Mount Vernon* during her war service, came out of the war in much better condition. Con-

Opposite Until the advent of the superliner *United States* in the summer of 1952, the *America* was the largest passenger ship in the US merchant marine. (*Alexanderson Collection*)

A typical departure scene: visitors crowd the outer end balcony of New York's Pier 61, for the 29 January 1949 sailing of the *America*. (*Alexanderson Collection*)

sequently, serious consideration was given to restoring her to peacetime luxury standards to operate alongside the *America*. Second thoughts prevailed, however, and she was refurbished as an austerity liner, carrying 1,106 passengers, all in low-fare tourist class quarters. She was refitted at the Newport News yard during 1947 and was later delivered to United States Lines. Although painted in commercial colours, she was not used, or even advertised, as a running mate of the far fancier *America*. 'Lots of the original furniture and woodwork were the same,' recalled Captain Robert Brooks, who began serving in the restored *Washington* in February 1948. 'The only difference was the dining room, which was still quite bare, as if in her war days. She was a very busy ship in those days, almost always carrying over 1,000 passengers per trip, to Cobh, Le Havre, Southampton and Hamburg (later changed to Bremerhaven). There were refugees and dependants and even some troops.'

Several years later, during 1952, Commodore Alexander son noted that the United States Lines ran four passenger ships and that this was the last time this would occur. 'We had the brand new *United States* and the *America*, of course, both on regular runs. Then there was also the *Washington* and the chartered *La Guardia* (a rebuilt former troopship that had been operated in the late 1940s by American Export Lines as a commercial liner on the Mediterranean run). Both

The classic scene from the deck of an outbound liner at New York. This Lower Manhattan scene includes two ships of the United Fruit Co as well as the Irving Trust, Bank of Manhattan, and Cities Service towers. (*Alexanderson Collection*)

of these ships were carrying dependants. The *Washington* continued to sail to Europe while the *La Guardia* sailed mostly to San Juan. The *United States* and *America* were treated separately and used our Hudson River passenger berths, at Pier 86. The *Washington* and *La Guardia* used the Brooklyn Army Base. The contract to carry dependants soon expired, however, and those two austerity-style ships later went into mothballs.'

The *Washington* had no further active life. She joined her sister in the upper Hudson River Reserve Fleet, remaining there until 1965, when she too was sold to Kearny, New Jersey scrappers, and broken up. The *La Guardia* later went to the Pacific and found further service with the newly-formed Hawaiian Textron Lines. She became their *Leilani* for San Francisco-Honolulu service. Unsuccessful, she later joined American President Lines and became their *President Roosevelt* in 1960. A decade later, as US-flag passenger shipping dwindled further because of increasingly high operational costs as well as recurrent labour difficulties, she was sold to foreign buyers, the Chandris Group of Greece, and was rebuilt yet again (her fourth major transformation no less) as the Caribbean cruiseship *Atlantis*. But, as in the past, her original 1944 troopship design—with such defence features as extra hull plating—meant that she was very hard on fuel and therefore a costly ship to operate. And so she was sold again, in 1972, to the Eastern Steamship Lines of Miami and raised the Panamanian flag. She became the *Emerald Seas* for the short-distance runs (requiring less speed and thus reducing the fuel problem) between Florida and the Bahamas. In this service, she has been a great and continuing success. (1990 was her forty-sixth year.)

In the late 1940s, the United States Lines operated several

The classically beautiful lines of the outbound *America* are set against that same Lower Manhattan skyline. It is late afternoon as the ship leaves her Chelsea berth. (*Alexanderson Collection*)

SS United States

comparatively austere passenger ships on the Atlantic. All of them were part of the wartime C4-Marine Class. Their design was noteworthy for the time: engines, and therefore funnels, placed aft. At some 12,500 tons each, they carried approximately 900 tourist class passengers. They retained their designated wartime names: *Marine Flasher, Marine Perch, Ernie Pyle, Marine Marlin, Marine Falcon, Marine Jumper, Marine Tiger, Marine Shark,* and *Marine Swallow*. Mostly, they made trips to war-ravaged Germany, to either Bremerhaven or Hamburg, and occasionally called in at Le Havre and Southampton. There were also periodically extended special trips, often in conjunction with the American Scantic Line, a subsidiary of the better known Moore McCormack Lines, to such northern ports as Gothenburg, Oslo, Copenhagen, and Gdynia. Captain Robert Brooks served in the *Ernie Pyle* in 1948: 'These ships were actually troopers placed on the peacetime North Atlantic, carrying dependants and refugees mostly. Actually, they were rather nice ships in their own way and were noted for having quite excellent food.' The sailings for this group, at least as part of the United States Lines, ended by the summer of 1948. Later mothballed, they were finally declared surplus by their owners, the US government, and then, because of their solid hulls and solid steam turbine machinery, found new careers as extensively converted container cargo ships. Now, of course,

Far left Famous visitors aboard the *America*: Mrs Harry Truman, wife of the then American President; Commodore John W. Anderson, then master of the United States Lines flagship; and Margaret Truman, daughter of the President and First Lady. (*Alexanderson Collection*)

Below far left Officers pose aboard the *America* in the fall of 1947. (*Alexanderson Collection*)

Below Inbound aboard the *America*. This view of her wheelhouse includes Captain Alexanderson on the far left and Commodore Anderson in the centre. (*Alexanderson Collection*)

nearly fifty years after their original creation, they have gone to the breakers.

However, on her own for some years without a proper running mate, the *America* prospered. She was solidly booked for her North Atlantic passages in the late forties. The tourist business was just beginning to revive and there was also a busy trade with businessmen, government officials, and their families. They used the liners then as they use the first and business class compartments of today's airliners. 'The *America* had very nice appointments,' recalled Commodore Alexanderson. 'She had some very attractive public rooms, such as her double-deck lounge and her main ballroom. She also had some very nice staterooms, many of which were so much larger than some of the rather cramped quarters offered in today's mega-cruiseships.'

C.M. Squarey, the noted British connoisseur of passenger ships, cast his expert eye over the *America* for the first time in March 1950. In his extensive journals, he wrote: 'Most people board a ship with certain expectations in mind. I expected this ship would conform to what I might call the American pattern; in my view, however, to call her a typical American ship would be wrong, yet there is quite enough

High style on the high seas: the superbly decorated first-class restaurant aboard the *America*. (*United States Lines*)

Opposite Happy days on the North Atlantic: shuffleboard aboard the eastbound *America*, in 1948. (*Alexanderson Collection*)

LIFEBOAT STATION № 12

The enclosed promenade deck as the *America* prepares to arrive at Cobh in Ireland. (*Alexanderson Collection*)

about her to remind you that she is, at heart, a "Yankee" ship—and that, indeed, is how she should be. Two women were entirely responsible for her furnishing. I pay this liner the compliment, by my code, of saying that she has got the glamour; rather has she the greater asset of irresistible attraction based on sophisticated charm. She blends very nicely restraint with progress; she incorporates a very modern approach to problems with just the right touch of respect for the older school.'

Operationally, the *America* was noted as a 'solid' ship. 'Of course, as a seaboat,' recalled Commodore Alexanderson, 'she didn't have the speed of the *United States*. Being shorter, she would slow herself down. Actually, she was a little too short in the bow and always had to be slowed down in foul weather. She was never quite as fast as Newport News said (24 knots), but actually she was the fastest 22-knot ship I ever saw!'

Commodore Alexanderson recalled one of her worst storms, encountered while eastbound from New York to Cobh, in January 1947. 'We reduced speed as was the customary practice. The ship's photographer came to the bridge, requesting permission to take pictures. Almost at the same time, the ship put her nose down and took a sea that carried away the two 10-ton booms that we had. One swung over the side, the other over the other boom. The boom on the port swung over the starboard boom. The starboard boom was out and swinging free. Crew were called and the boom was secured with lines. Once back at New York, the forward bulwarks were cut back and pipe rails fitted so that the ship could free herself more quickly of water. A deck anchor had been lifted out of its moorings as well. The weight of the water even buckled the stanchions below the deck.'

Each winter, the *America* would go to the Newport News shipyards for a month-long overhaul. There was the customary painting, repair work, and general house cleaning. Commodore Alexanderson had a special recollection during one of these drydock periods. 'I had been working all day, until about 6 pm. Bill Kolbe, the Chief Engineer, and I decided to go ashore to a Washington Avenue diner for a steak dinner (a good steak was then $4!), but the steaks were inedible. The waitress took them back, but the seconds were just as bad. We refused to pay the bill. The manager told a story to a policeman, who just happened to be there as well. The manager insisted that we should be arrested. They asked for our names. The next day, the chief of security for Newport News Shipyard, Bill Metts, appeared with a local police lieutenant, who had warrants for two crewmembers. I asked for their names and the lieutenant said

Perfect service: a steward attends to Governor Thomas E. Dewey of New York, on Voyage No 44, June 1949.
(*Alexanderson Collection*)

Alexanderson and Kolbe. If we paid up, the matter would be straightened out. Those two steaks cost us $25 apiece. They were the most expensive steaks I ever had. Bill Metts is now a neighbour of ours in Hampton.'

Even after the spectacular arrival of the *United States* in July 1952, and with her instant and enormous popularity ('Everyone wanted to sail in her, especially in those days,' recalled noted maritime historian Frank O. Braynard), the smaller and slower *America* managed to hold her own for some years. Oddly, she was also a suspicious ship for some time. 'We were inbound for New York,' remembered Commodore Alexanderson, 'when the chief officer discovered lots of rather odd boxes. There were about 98 of them. They contained illegal Irish Sweepstake tickets and receipts. The US Customs and even the FBI were notified when we reached New York. While they might have been thrown overboard, the crew seemed to be unaware of them. A big investigation followed. The chief storekeeper, who had bought them at Cobh and was forced to keep them by the Mafia, had to accept responsibility. He was innocent, but had been forced— threatened with "floating in the harbour". He went to prison for a year and afterward there were investigations aboard the *America* for some time. It was all very sad. When

Above far left January 1947: the *America* encounters one of her worst storms. (*Alexanderson Collection*)

Far left The starboard boom is ripped loose in the ferocious North Atlantic winter storm. (*Alexanderson Collection*)

Above A brave and skilled photographer captured this view during that same 1947 storm. (*Alexanderson Collection*)

Safe arrival: the *America* is berthed at Southampton's Ocean Terminal. The British troopship *Asturias*, a former Royal Mail Lines passenger liner, is to the left. (*Alexanderson Collection*)

that storekeeper was finally released, he went to tankers.'

Like most big Atlantic liners, the *America* was affected, in 1958-9, by the sudden and very dramatic appearance of the first commercial jets. First, her winter crossings were hit—there were simply less and less passengers. United States Lines managers wanted to resume winter cruises to the Caribbean, the first in nearly a decade and certainly the ideal economic alternative. Unfortunately, the US government in the form of the all-powerful Maritime Administration, which controlled the vital subsidies given not only to the *America* but to the *United States* as well, refused to allow cruising. Such tropical trips, so those Washington bureaucrats insisted, were in violation of the subsidy rules. American passenger ships could not deviate from their prescribed services. It seemed, at least at first, that such rules were carved in stone.

Finally, in 1961, the Maritime Administration relented and altered the rules. The *America* would be allowed to make her first off-season cruise. It was a five-day trip over the long Thanksgiving holiday weekend that November. Minimum fares started at $145. More cruises followed, and soon after for the *United States* as well; but the general picture, the overall forecasts and thickening problems, was not particularly bright. Operational costs were steadily rising—and at an alarming rate—against diminishing profits, the situation complicated further by increasingly frequent strikes and labour problems. The biggest blow, and perhaps the most significant turning-point not only for the *America* but for the *United States* as well, occurred in September 1963. Just before a noontime Saturday sailing to Europe, a labour problem erupted on board the *America*—a racial problem to do with the use of a lavatory. Some of the crew suddenly refused to sail unless it was properly resolved—and quickly. Meanwhile, the United States Lines' management—with the prospect of ever reducing profit ahead on a steadily declining Atlantic run—lost patience with yet another labour complication. They reacted almost immediately: the voyage was cancelled and the ship was to be laid up, at least for the winter season ahead. Amidst the shock, surprise, and even anger of some crewmembers, there were rumours that the *America* would never sail again under the Stars and Stripes. There were even whispers that the United States Lines were grateful for the labour unrest, which gave them a perfect excuse to retire the ship.

Disappointed, unhappy, and with their plans disrupted, the *America*'s passengers were sent ashore. With their crossing cancelled, they were reassigned mostly to other foreign-flag liners, a few to the next sailing of the *United States*, and—

A tender approaches the 723-ft long *America* at Cobh. (*Alexanderson Collection*)

Below Southampton's
Western Docks, in
August 1949: the
Cunarder *Mauretania* is
stern-to-stern with the
American flagship.
(*Alexanderson Collection*)

Bottom The revived,
but austerity-class
Washington as seen
from the *America* off
the Irish coast. The
date is 13 September
1949. (*Alexanderson
Collection*)

and worst of all—some to the airlines! These labour problems, and those frequent and numerous strikes that had
been troubling American liner firms for some time, further
tarnished the image of both the *America* and the *United States*.
A sort of slow death and decay had begun. It was all a matter of time. A small fleet of tugs towed the *America* from her
berth at Pier 86 across the Hudson to the Todd Shipyards
in Hoboken, New Jersey. Silent and unlit by night, only security and basic maintenance was in force. She sat there—sad
and with an uncertain future—for the next six months,
through that long winter, sometimes with her outer decks
littered with snow.

The *America* did resume her Atlantic schedule in the spring
of 1964, but the rumours were mounting. Indeed, her United
States Lines' days were numbered. That August, just as the

Master's Birth Certificate

S. S. America

Captain L. J. Alexanderson
Captain, U.S.N.R.

Voyage 123, Westbound — Sailing from:
Bremerhaven, Saturday, February 6th, 1954, via Havre, Southampton and Cobh
Arriving at New York, Tuesday, February 16th, 1954

THIS IS TO CERTIFY THAT AT 1350 HOURS THIS DAY, FEBRUARY 14, 1954 AT LATITUDE 41 DEGREES, 56 MINUTES NORTH AND LONGITUDE 59 DEGREES, 15 MINUTES WEST, A MALE CHILD, 7 POUNDS (AULDEN) WAS BORN TO PASSENGER, PATRICIA BADENHOP, AGE 18, U.S. CITIZEN OF 1392 MOUNTAIN VIEW AVENUE, PETALUMA, CALIFORNIA. PASSENGER WAS ACCOMPANIED BY HUSBAND, ALVIN BADENHOP.

Surgeon   Master

1965 sailing schedule was to be released, the formal news came out of 1 Broadway in Lower Manhattan: the *America* would be retired in November. The rumours, as is often the case, had proved all too true. The demise of this ship under the American colours was also the gradual beginning of the end of all US-owned liners in transatlantic service. On 9 October she left New York on her last roundtrip crossing. The *New York Times* reported on this event:

The liner *America* is to sail today on her last voyage for the United States Lines. When the 24-year-old former queen of the country's merchant marine returns on October 29th from North Atlantic ports, she may be towed to a scrapyard or sold to a foreign-flag operator. While the company had no comment and has not made formal application to the Maritime Administration to cancel the ship's three other scheduled sailings this year, officials of some of the unions represented said they had 'got the word'.

At her home berth at Pier 86 at West 46th Street and the Hudson River, an official of Local 824 of the International Longshoremen's Association said about 300 dockworkers would lose about $3,000 a year, or half of their annual wages for loading and unloading the *America*. The National Maritime Union, with about 600 seamen employed on the ship, said no official word had been received. However, many crewmembers were convinced last night that this was the ship's last sailing.

About 12 employees of the United States Lines' passenger department were reported to have been given notice of termination of employment as of November 1st. An official of A.L. Burbank & Co Ltd, ship agent and broker, said in August that negotiations for the sale of the *America* to the Chandris shipping interests of Greece were continuing. Yesterday, a company spokes-

The liner *America* berthed across from the aircraft carrier *America* at the Newport News yards. Note the *United States* at the opposite end of the shipyard. (*Alexanderson Collection*)

man indicated that there might be a development soon, but declined to comment further. Reports also were widespread in shipping circles that the great ship might be sold for scrap, but again the company had no comment.

Ironically, as the *America* was retired, so was her master, Captain Frederick Fender. On 1 November the *New York Herald Tribune* noted the retirement of both ship and master.

It is but fitting that this opportunity be taken to render
A salute to the *America*'s commander, Captain Frederick Fender,
Whose retirement coinciding with the lay-up is so intertwined,
As to confirm the ship and master are happily combined.
Good luck, good health and happiness to you,
Is the wish of officers and ratings who comprise the crew;
Like your ship, your course too, has been well run,
And with her we give you, 'Hip, Hip, Hooray', and a rousing,
'Well done'.

The above two stanzas of a poem were dedicated to Captain Frederick Fender when his ship, the liner *America*, was withdrawn last Tuesday from American flag service. The author of the poem was Cecil W. Phillips, a steward of the *America*'s cocktail lounge for the last six years. Captain Fender retired yesterday, ending a half century of seafaring.

The relationship between the master of a big passenger liner like the *America* and members of her crew is of necessity formal. But Captain Fender, during the nine years he commanded the nation's second largest passenger ship, gained the affection of most of the regular crew. They were almost as saddened to see him 'swallow the anchor' (maritime language for retire) as they were to see the *America* withdrawn last week from transatlantic service under the American flag for sale to Greek interests. Mr Phillips said yesterday he had penned his six-stanza poem during the *America*'s last voyage. The first four stanzas were devoted to the ship; the last two to her commander. 'We all liked the captain,' said Mr Phillips. 'He ran a happy ship.'

There had been many rumours about the fate of the *America*, including 'mothball reserve' by the government or perhaps even scrapping. But the Chandris Group offered the irresistible price: $6.3 million and for a 24-year-old liner. The ship went down to the Newport News yards for her final decommissioning, a last check by the Greek engineers and then—with the contract signed and in hand—her funnels were repainted in Chandris colours, her new name stencilled on the bow and stern, and the colours of Greece hoisted (then being the largest ship under that flag). She was renamed *Australis*, which translated to 'Australian maiden', an appropriate choice for her new life: service between Europe and Australia with immigrants and low-fare tourists. 'On her last sailing from Newport News,' remembered Commodore Alexanderson, 'I couldn't go. It was too sad to see her in Greek colours.'

She crossed first to Greek waters and there, at an anchorage at Perama not far from Piraeus, she was rebuilt. Instead of the customary drydock or shipyard berth, she was kept at anchor and the work fed by barges and workboats. This saved considerable money for Chandris and the teams also included some that would serve aboard the ship. Consequently, her crew and her engineers would be familiar with everything about her. The biggest task was doubling her capacity, from 1,046 to an almost amazing 2,258. Some cabins were divided, others added, and some of the crew quarters were reallocated as passenger space. The original class distinctions disappeared in favour of an all tourist class configuration. She was given air conditioning throughout, to cope with those steamy passages through Suez, the Red Sea, and the Indian Ocean, and a large outdoor pool was fitted aft. In all, the Chandris conversion, with the accountants closely scrutinizing the expenses, cost $5.6 million. Most likely, this would have been double had it been done in a conventional shipyard.

The *Australis* set off on her first trip, in August 1965. Thereafter, her customary routing was on three-month trips around the world: Bremerhaven, Rotterdam, Southampton, Casablanca, Las Palmas, Capetown (or through the Mediterranean via Gibraltar, Naples, Malta, Piraeus, Port Said, and Aden), Fremantle, Melbourne, Sydney, Auckland, Suva, Tahiti, Acapulco, Balboa, Cristobal, Port Everglades, and return to Southampton. She also cruised on occasion—from Southampton to the Canary Islands, Spain and Portugal, West Africa and sometimes into the Mediterranean. The prices were just right for the times—£84 in September 1972, for 14 days from Southampton to Barcelona, Tangier, Gibraltar, Lanzarote, Teneriffe, Madeira, and Lisbon.

Chandris had the Australian government's prized migrant contract, bringing scores of low-fare (often as little as £10) settlers out to Fremantle, Melbourne, and Sydney. This usually meant that she was 'sold out' to every last berth (and especially with families and 'shares' in the larger 4- and 6-berth cabins on the lower decks). One staff member later recalled: 'Those outward sailings were often so crowded that we had to have three sittings for dinner and usually one just for the 500 or so children that might be aboard.'

The *Australis* had just over a decade of extremely profitable service on the Down Under run. In 1977, however, Chandris lost that government migrant contract (thereafter, they would all go by the inevitable jet) and so, in that Novem-

Opposite The *America's* clean bow lines and hull form are well seen in this view in a Newport News dry dock. (*Newport News Shipbuilding & Dry Dock Co*)

ber, she made her last trip out to Sydney. Afterward, she was laid up, at an anchorage in rather remote Timaru in New Zealand. There was again uncertainty, as there had been in 1964 when she was to be retired by the Americans, about her future. Some believed that she would now make only one further voyage: up to the Far East, to those ever-hungry scrappers of Kaohsiung on Taiwan.

In the spring of 1978, however, and with the hope of cashing-in on the short cruise business out of US East Coast ports, especially from New York, several American business-men, all of them owning travel agencies, offered to buy the idle *Australis* for $5 million. The offer was promptly accepted and so she was 'steamed up' and sailed via Panama for New York. Once there, in late May, she was sent to the big grav-ing dock at Bayonne, New Jersey (used by her on occasion in earlier days as the *America* and also by the *United States*, and later that same year by the *Queen Elizabeth 2*), which had been leased by the Navy to the Bethlehem Steel Com-pany's ship repair division. The hull and machinery were said to be in very fine condition—a great testament to her original construction some forty years before. Otherwise, little else was done. The investors were satisfied and again the final sale contracts were signed. Then, and as irrever-ent as it seemed to some, the new owners decided to rename her as *America*, to capitalize on the ship's illustrious earlier heritage. Her new operators were even listed as American Cruise Lines, but a small, Connecticut-based operation, which ran coastal cruiseships, objected (and in court) and so the *America*'s new owners were soon relisted as Venture Cruise Lines.

The schedule of short cruises—three days to 'nowhere', four and five days up to Halifax, and five days to Nassau—barely began when there were problems, in fact very serious problems. In June, just before her inaugural trip, I went aboard the liner, which was, unusually, being 'refitted' at a regular passenger berth, at New York's Pier 92, at the foot of West 52nd Street. In earlier days, that terminal had been used by Cunard and was now part of the new six-berth con-solidated cruise centre. Once aboard, most noticeable was the ship's near filthy condition: small mountains of soiled linens and masses of well-used mattresses, scattered bundles of rubbish and, just about everywhere, in every passage and corridor, a stale stench—a foul mixture of kitchen odours, engine oils, and plumbing backups. A gaseous odour usually comes from the pipes in older liners, and the *America* was no exception. Evidently, there had been some rundown and deferred maintenance even in her final Chandris passenger

Her second life: the restyled *America* as the Australian migrant ship *Australis* of Chandris Lines. (*Alex Duncan*)

Stripped of her forward funnel and in a deteriorated condition, the idle *Australis* is seen at Eleusis in Greece, in June 1986. Another Chandris liner, the *Ellinis*, the former Matson *Lurline* of 1931, is seen to the right. (*Antonio Scrimali*)

Two years later, in June 1988, a large oil drilling platform is nested alongside the rusted ex-*America*. (*Antonio Scrimali*)

days. It seemed so unfitting for a once glittering liner. The decks were also in deep decay, suffering all the ill effects of long overdue maintenance. There was rust, leaking water from overhead pipes, even holes caused by corrosion in the 'dummy' forward funnel. Noticeably, there were far too many layers of paint slapped over the outer bulk heads, on the rails and—most alarmingly—on the davits and lifeboat gear. College students, employed at minimum labour rates, were rather carelessly painting some of the public rooms. The once impeccable stainless trims, for example, were scarred by brush strokes. Most obviously, the ship needed weeks, if not months, of overhaul at a proper shipyard. Alternatively, it seemed that she might best be sent on to the scrappers.

On 30 June, however, and booked with some 900 passengers that responded to the glowing and spirited newspaper advertising by Venture Cruise Lines, and by the $75-a-day rates, she set off on her first cruise—a trip to nowhere. A near-mutiny followed, with reports of inadequate food, plumbing problems, untrained staff members, uncleanliness, and, perhaps most horrifying, reports of rats and cockroaches seen throughout the passenger areas. Somehow, she managed a second cruise, a five-day trip up to Halifax, but the same complaints—plus reports of garbage being stored in the outdoor pool—surfaced. The publicity was deadly; the old *America* was defaced, ruined. Her owners had already incurred over $500,000 worth of fines. Promptly, Venture Cruise Lines closed its doors and declared bankruptcy.

The worn-out, scarred *America* spent the remaining weeks of that 1978 summer at her Pier 92 berth. Some onlookers occasionally thought of earlier days, of better times for the ship, when there had been those colourful and splendid gatherings of passenger ships along 'Luxury Liner Row'. Now she sat— lifeless, dark, and seemingly hopeless—as other liners came and went from adjacent berths. In late August, the New York City Bankruptcy Court marshals and their agents went aboard and, in view of her debts, auctioned off the 38-year-old liner. Surprisingly, the buyers were Chandris and the price was an amazing $1 million, or $4 million less than the amount for which they sold her four months earlier. A skeleton crew was mustered and, on 6 September, and largely unnoticed, the *America* slipped out of New York, for the last time, bound for Piraeus.

Again, the ship was moored in Perama Bay, in those extraordinary but rather haphazard anchorages and nestings of ships owned by Greek shippers. Some of her neighbours at the time included well- known passenger ships: the Chandris liner *Ellinis*, the former Norwegian America *Bergensfjord*, the Greek Line's *Olympia*, Furness Bermuda's former *Ocean Monarch*, and, among the oldest of all, Grace Line's onetime *Santa Paula* of 1932. There seemed little hope for some ships, but there were further repairs made to the *America* and then, with her forward funnel removed, she reappeared as the *Italis*—'the Italian lady'—for charter Mediterranean cruises out of Barcelona. But this too was short lived. By the autumn of 1979 she was once more out of service and was again at her moorings in Perama Bay. Her commercial sailing days, it seemed, were over.

She has remained there, steadily decaying, ever since. There have been rumours, of course, as with her former fleet-mate *United States*. It is ironic that the two biggest American transatlantic liners are enduring extended lay-ups, both of them in limbo. There were reports that the *America* would become a hotelship in a West African port, a 'floating prison' at Galveston, Texas, and one wildly enthusiastic report indicated that she would return to the New York waterfront but as a greatly restored 'luxury hotel'—the Hotel *America*! In 1980, she was transferred to Intercommerce Corporation SA, presumably an intermediary firm, and renamed *Noga*. The next change, in 1984, was to Silver Moon Ferries Ltd, who renamed her once again, this time as *Alferdoss*. Little else has happened to her. In 1988, however, and as the scrappers (from Turkey, Pakistan, India, and even China) began to file their bids, there were worrisome troubles for the 723-ft long liner. In October, her hull ruptured, there was flooding and then a list; finally, she had to be beached on the shores of Perama Bay. If nothing else, this should prompt her owners to take a decision on her final fate and finish off the old *America*. One day, perhaps, her story will be told in full.

Chapter 3

Creation of a Superliner

William Francis Gibbs was a genius. He was the greatest of all American naval architects. Certainly, his finest work was the SS *United States*, a ship said by many, both friend and critic alike of Gibbs, to be the most technologically advanced ocean liner ever built. She was the wonder ship of her time and, to many, remains unequalled—even though she has finished her second decade in lay-up, in solitude and isolation. The combination of the brilliance of Gibbs and the manifestation of his extraordinary skills, abilities, and foresight in the *United States* project represented an ultimate union. Frank O. Braynard, the well-known maritime artist, writer, and historian, said it so well in his own book, *The Big Ship: The Story of the SS United States*, published in 1981: 'Supership, superman and super merger of the two!'

Gibbs began drawing ships at the age of three. He was fascinated by them, by their form and shape, and by their evolution. He loved them with a deepening passion. As a youngster, in the 1890s, he had something of a crow's nest view. His family summered along the New Jersey shore, at a resort known as Spring Lake. On the clearest days, when visibility extended for miles, he could peer across the distant waters to the very mouth of New York harbour where he could see the silhouettes of the greatest and grandest liners of the day.

When he was just eight years old, in November 1894, William Francis and his beloved brother Frederic had the good fortune to be invited to the Cramp Shipyards in Philadelphia. It was a special occasion: the launching of the new liner *St Louis*. She was for the American Line and, at nearly 12,000 tons, she would be one of the largest, most important passenger ships of her time. But even more intriguing to the fiercely patriotic Gibbs brothers, she would fly the Stars and Stripes and in doing so challenge 'those foreigners'.

Quite incidentally, the American Line would eventually lead to the creation of the United States Lines, the same company that would operate the *United States*, Gibbs' dream ship. Furthermore, that festive launching at Philadelphia prompted a deep promise from the young boy. On that day—earning the gratitude of seamen, passengers, and ship buffs ever since—the 8-year-old genius vowed to dedicate his life to ships. Those impressions of the *St Louis* never left him.

He sketched liners, kept notebooks and diaries about them, filled scrapbooks with pictures and newspaper articles, and eventually began to think of a ship of his own. He was fascinated by speed and size and, more specifically, by such design ingredients as large funnels. He always felt that liners had to convey a sense of power and might.

Rather oddly, however, Gibbs took a law degree in 1913

Unveiling: the first glimpse of the SS *United States*, at the Gibbs & Cox offices in New York City, on 5 April 1948. William Francis Gibbs is at the head of the table, just off to the right, his hand placed behind his head. Also note that the model includes an additional set of aft king posts as well as an extra blue band on the funnels. (*Frank O. Braynard Collection*)

Some of the first steel sections going into place for the new American flagship. The date is August 1950. (*Frank O. Braynard Collection*)

and then began graduate studies in—again rather oddly— economics. But his fascination for, and his extraordinary skills with, ships remained an all engrossing hobby. When away from his law studies, his mind often wandered— particularly to transatlantic speed record-breakers that would be as much as 1,000 feet long. It was inevitable: Gibbs soon lost interest in the law and turned to ships and ship design as a career. Together with his brother Frederic the pair formed their own naval architectural firm, the Gibbs Brothers Company. The doors opened in 1916, the year before America entered the First World War.

The Company was built up steadily. In 1921 they were contracted to convert the German liner *Vaterland*, a war prize, into the American *Leviathan*, and this became a testing-ground for many of Gibbs' superliner theories. But their Lower New York City offices were also kept busy with cargo ships and warships, even fireboats and ferries. Later, they won several very important passenger ship contracts. Matson Line's *Malolo* of 1927 was not only the first big luxury ship to be built for the California-Hawaii run, she was also one of the safest ships afloat. Shipboard safety had been another of Gibbs' fascinations. Later, in 1932-3, the Gibbs Company produced a superb quartet of little liners for the

Grace Line: the *Santa Rosa, Santa Paula, Santa Elena* and *Santa Lucia*. But it was some three years later, in 1936, that the glowing reputation of William Francis Gibbs won for him the most important American shipbuilding contract of the decade.

The newly-created US Maritime Commission planned to revitalize the fading national merchant marine and proposed a new North Atlantic liner. She would be called *America* and Gibbs was selected to design her. She was to be the national flagship and certainly one of the very finest liners of her day. At nearly 34,000 tons, though neither a speed champion nor statistical recordbreaker, she would rank as the largest liner yet built in the United States. Otherwise, she was in almost every way the 'dry run', as Frank Braynard called her, for that ultimate supership, that great speed challenger, that remained in Gibbs' mind. He felt more assured than ever: she might be built in the early 1940s.

But as the *America* was nearing completion and the superliner project was nothing more than a series of plans, the Second World War erupted and most passenger ship projects were pushed aside. Beginning in the autumn of 1939, Gibbs' full attention and that of his entire firm turned to the war effort: building cargo ships, revitalizing others, conversion projects, and major repair works. In all, between 1940 and

Building what will become the mightiest funnels of the day. (*Newport News Shipbuilding & Dry Dock Co*)

1945, the Gibbs Company, which had been renamed as Gibbs & Cox, produced the design or plans for nearly two-thirds of all merchant ships built in those years and for nearly three-quarters of all warships. What an exceptionally, almost mind-bogglingly productive period!

Somehow the ideas, plans, and overall projections for the so-called 'big ship', as she came to be known, remained alive despite those hectic and pressuring war years. Several reports indicate that the first official drawings and designs were started in 1943-4, but that certain other specifications were prepared as early as 1940. Generally, the overall concepts could still be traced back to 1915, to speed queens with exceptional 30-knot capabilities that Gibbs had planned but that never quite materialized. But in the Second World War, the stage was set: the US government saw superliners in a far different, more encouraging light.

By the end of the war, War Department officials were overwhelmingly impressed by the exceptional success of Cunard's mighty *Queen Mary* and *Queen Elizabeth* as troopships. Their size meant that their peacetime capacities could be expanded to over seven times the intended number (from approximately 2,000 to 15,000 each) and their speeds (in excess of 28 knots) allowed them to outpace the lethal Nazi U-boats. Their records were superb. The US government had paid for their wartime trooping operations on the Atlantic, however, and so—coupled with the potential of transatlantic commercial service—the mood moved closer and closer to building at least one Yankee superliner. In 1946, with the war over and with the *Queens* being returned to Cunard for refitting and return to liner service, the US government considered its future needs for a troopship-liner. Another war—particularly in the threatening era of the Cold War—was entirely possible and Washington questioned the wisdom of relying again on big foreign liners. In fact, in October 1944, before the war had even ended, and with the personal support of President Franklin D. Roosevelt, big new American passenger liners were very much under consideration. Plans soon became far more ambitious and were said to include no less than eleven superliners for peacetime services on routes around the world. They would also be among the fastest and safest ships anywhere. The first pair was to have speeds of 29 knots and were intended for the Atlantic run.

This scheme for eleven liners was reworked and later reduced considerably, especially as the government's priori-

Nearly complete: the *United States* in the spring of 1952. (*Mariners Museum*)

ties began to change in the immediate post-war years. There were also those who began to be aware of the distant threat of that rapidly developing technological rival: the airliner. But trans-ocean passenger airliners were still a rather remote challenge in 1946 and the plans for at least one big Atlantic liner—fortunately, the Gibbs' speed champion—were not affected by the change in mood. While the first large-scale planning was done as early as 1943, the United States Lines—the only American passenger ship firm seriously interested in such a ship and with the experience of operating her—authorized further planning in 1946. There had already been considerable discussions with the United States Lines and the US government on this 'big ship' project. A marriage of sorts had taken place shortly after the war: the government would build and pay for most of her, the United States Lines would own (under lease) and operate her.

Gibbs & Cox and the United States Lines also began discussions for another liner, a slightly larger version of the *America*. This ship would be about 40,000 tons and 790 ft in length but would have an exceptionally high speed of 30 knots. The plans were soon abandoned, however, when it was revealed that such a high speed could not be maintained, at least comfortably, by a vessel of that length. Again,

Opposite Lunch hour at the shipyard! (*Newport News Shipbuilding & Dry Dock Co*)

A stern view of the soon-to-be-christened *United States*. The big graving dock has been completely flooded. (*Frank O. Braynard Collection*)

the 'big ship' project endured—perhaps even more importantly than ever.

The general agreement, at least by late 1945, between the government and the United States Lines, then gradually resuming its commercial operations, was that 'a great ship should be built primarily for the national defense of the United States and we would try to combine in such a design the requirements of a passenger ship'. The United States Lines' management actually wanted two superliners, in particular for a weekly service similar to the one Cunard was about to begin with the restored *Queens* in 1947. But this too was reviewed and then reduced to a single giant liner. Many others, particularly in Washington, thought that one ship would be more economically sound. Two liners would be pure luxury and far less profitable. In hindsight, they were quite right.

Christening day and the inevitable speeches. (*Mariners Museum*)

The official baptism!
(*Newport News Shipbuilding & Dry Dock Co*)

Thereafter, the plan was for the new superliner to operate with the *America*, then about to be refitted following war duties as a troop transport, and with the older *Washington*, on the assumption that it would be fully restored (it was later reappraised and revived only as an austerity-style passenger ship). More specifically, according to at least one detailed plan, the *Washington* was to be used as a luxury passenger ship until 1956 (or thereabouts) and then a second superliner would be built. Obviously, this scheme never came to pass either. Overall, the philosophy at United States Lines was 'to develop and build the greatest passenger ship in the world'. At Gibbs & Cox, according to Frank Braynard's thorough research, 'The new liner was a synthesis of all the experiences gained by Gibbs & Cox from passenger ships such as the *Leviathan*, the *Malolo*, the four Grace liners and the *America*, of course, and then combined with the technical advances made in machinery, structure, materials and methods developed in their work for the US Navy. The new ship had to be the safest afloat, with standards of subdivision and fire resistance surpassing all others. She had to compete with the two British *Queen*s in luxury, accommodation and to be much faster—and all this at less fuel consumption. And, she had to be at the same time convertible to a troopship.' Furthermore, she was expected to give the

85

The great liner is moved, her first official trip, from the graving dock to the fitting-out berth. (*Mariners Museum*)

competitive edge to the Americans on the North Atlantic for at least the next twenty years.

Planning and additional studies, research, and the inevitable meetings with the government and the United States Lines kept Gibbs & Cox very busy. As war work ebbed, greater attention was turned to this new passenger liner (by 1948, she would become the top priority at the designers' Lower Manhattan offices). There were all kinds of studies, tests, and revisions. One early plan, for example, called for a new United States Lines' service: New York to Plymouth, England and then Flushing, Holland before returning via Southampton to New York. Another proposal was for United States Lines to have only two classes—first and tourist. But the government resisted, realizing that the new ship would also be used, at least on periodic crossings, to carry military dependents and perhaps even some servicemen. Such passengers could be carried in tourist class, leaving two classes for other passengers: luxurious first class and less expensive but still comfortable cabin class. The government won out in the end.

Soon, however, much of the general planning would be veiled in tight secrecy, the result of demands made by William Francis Gibbs himself. Officially, it was said that the secrecy was a result of the US Navy's special specifications for the liner, but in actuality it was Gibbs' almost furious jealousy to keep design and operational details from 'those foreign liners', particularly from the likes of Cunard. This intense secrecy (always a strong feature of Gibbs' character) persisted so that key design elements in the American superliner remained under wraps, and as late as 1962 were not even copied in the *France*.

Generally, the most prominent and promising features of the new superliner were to be her extraordinary light weight, especially through the extensive use of aluminium throughout her entire superstructure, and her exceptional power—the greatest amount of horsepower ever to go into a liner. Planning moved ahead steadily and finally all agreements were in hand. On 5 April 1948, the press were invited to the Manhattan offices of Gibbs & Cox at 21 West Street. The model of the superliner was unveiled for the first time. Preliminary details revealed that she would be about 48,000 gross tons (compared to the 81,000 of the *Queen Mary* and 83,000 of the *Queen Elizabeth*), carry 2,000 passengers (about the same as the *Queen Mary*) and cost a startling $70,000,000 (compared to the likes of $24,000,000 for the *Queen Mary* less than twenty years before, in the mid 1930s, and $28,000,000 for the exquisite French *Normandie*, built in the same period). Soon after, three major US shipyards bid for the construction of the new ship: Newport News Shipbuilding & Dry Dock Co at Newport News, Virginia; the Bethlehem Steel Company at Quincy, Massachusetts; and the New York Shipbuilding Corporation at Camden, New Jersey. By December, the New York Shipbuilding Corporation had dropped out. Bethlehem Steel was more expensive than Newport News and with a longer construction timetable, and so Newport News won out—bidding $67.3 million and a 1,128-day schedule until delivery.

Gibbs soon insisted, in his position as construction supervisor, that the new liner should be built in a graving dock rather than in the more conventional slanted building slip. As far less of the actual hull construction would be exposed

The funnels dominate the still incomplete ship — note that none of the lifeboats are yet in place. (*Newport News Shipbuilding & Dry Dock Co*)

the details of the ship's construction had a greater chance of remaining secret.

The adjacent graving dock at Newport News was to be used for a new 65,000-ton aircraft carrier. It was at this time that rumours began—and persisted for some time thereafter—that the liner was actually intended to be a carrier. Captain Robert Brooks remembered this period:

The keel for that carrier, and said to be named *United States*, the first of the new generation of 'super carriers', was laid down but then soon cancelled. Congress had withdrawn the necessary funding. The name *United States* was then transferred to the emerging hull in the adjacent graving dock. Furthermore, the hull configurations of a liner and of an aircraft carrier are quite different. They are not the same. The hull of the SS *United States* could never have been intended for a carrier. There was also some later confusion as well. The power plants in the subsequent *Forrestal* class of aircraft carriers were the same as the one aboard the *United States*. Again, there were rumours that the liner *United States* was actually intended to be a carrier. But, because of the configuration of the carriers' hulls, they could manage about 36 knots whereas the *United States* could do at least 40 knots.

More studies, reviews, and revisions, and then final decisions were reached. For example, two women would design the passenger interiors because, as Mr Gibbs thought, over three-quarters of all tickets sold were through the recommendation of women. On another point, the exact number of the crew kept changing, as did the specific numbers of

High drama and thick smoke: the *United States* prepares to sail off on her first sea trials. The tug *George W. Stevens* of the Chesapeake & Ohio Railroad is in the foreground. (*Mariners Museum*)

passengers per class. The length was said to be 980 ft, but this would be extended by another 10 ft. The top speed was said to be 'about' 30 knots, but this was certainly a conservative estimate. Even the stacks would be changed and increased in height from the original plans. Mr Gibbs still loved big stacks!

Newport News listed her as Hull No 488. The choice of a name also sparked off many rumours. *Mayflower, Columbia*, and even *American Engineer* were bandied about. It was not until May 1949 that the selection was made. *United States* was the choice from the start, though it had initially been chosen by the Navy for their proposed super-carrier. It was only two weeks after the Navy cancelled their carrier plans, in the spring of 1948, that United States Lines made their formal selection. Not everyone thought well of it at first. Some thought a single-word name, more compatible with *America*, would have been more appropriate, something like *Hudson* or *Manhattan*.

Also during 1949, high post-war enthusiasm for new big American liners began to fade, and fade quickly. Some believed that the air age was imminent; others felt that the era of big troopships was over; still others, in the growing conservatism and perhaps even scepticism of the late 1940s, thought that extravagant government spending on liners should be watched closely. The high pitch of the wartime Roosevelt administration had certainly changed to the more cautious pace of the Truman period. Those projected eleven big liners of 1945-6 had withered down to six passenger ships by 1949: the 48,000-ton *United States* for the United States Lines; twin 29,000-ton sisters for American Export Lines, to be called *Constitution* and *Independence*; and then three 13,000-

Radiant, sleek, and brand new, the *United States* begins to race along the Virginia Capes. (*Newport News Shipbuilding & Dry Dock Co*)

Late afternoon silhouette: the day's test runs are all but complete. (*Newport News Shipbuilding & Dry Dock Co*)

ton combination passenger-cargo liners for American President, to be called *President Adams, President Jackson,* and *President Hayes.* The government would spend some $150,000,000 to build these ships, but it would cost only $70,000,000 for the three shipping firms to acquire them. Inevitably, there was some sentiment against these expensive ships.

The keel for the *United States* was laid down on 8 February 1950. A 55-ton section was the beginning of what was now being called a 50,000 ton liner. She had grown by 2,000 tons from the original projections made two years before. Then, quite suddenly, five months later, everything nearly changed. On 25 July the Korean War started and almost immediately there were rumours: would the new liner *United States* be completed as a troopship? Within weeks, during a very tense August, there were said to be specific reports that the Defense Department had asked how long it would take to complete the new ship as a trooper. There were even further reports, reviving earlier shipyard gossip, that she would be redesigned and finished as a carrier.

The bombshell fell in September. News was flashed, and this time it sounded official, that the government was taking the 50,000-ton ship as well as that trio of 13,000-tonners intended for American President Lines for use as emergency troop transports. The *United States* was a little less than a third complete at the time. The Associated Press conscientiously informed its subscribers, 'The *United States* will get a new name for military usage. It will carry 12,000 troops. The three President liners will also be renamed. They will carry up to 3,000 troops each.'

It was a particularly tense time—and very disappointing and disruptive to many. Gibbs & Cox, in particular William Francis himself, would be saddened to see her finished as a troopship instead of a glittering new liner. It was also a disappointment for United States Lines, busy with plans for her maiden season of crossings, as well as for the press, members of the travel industry, and even the general public, all of whom had been reading about the ship in periodic press releases.

But then came the good news. All was well again. Nearly seven weeks after the official US government decision had been announced, it was rescinded, on 1 November. Quite simply, she would be too expensive as a troopship, a dan-

Guests and crew share in the excitement of the speed trials. (*Mariners Museum*)

Another trial view, at Newport News, in May 1952. (*Newport News Shipbuilding & Dry Dock Co*)

A wonderfully dramatic view of the world's fastest liner, making over 38 knots and, for a short time, an incredible 43 knots! (*Frank O. Braynard Collection*)

Racing again — at nearly 40 knots! The ship's good looks are particularly apparent in this view. (*United States Lines*)

gerous target, and, in many parts of the Far East, she would be too large to go alongside, posing a major operational difficulty especially when 10-12,000 troops were involved. The intended American President ships were not released, however, and they became the troopers *Barrett* (ex-*President Jackson*), *Geiger* (ex-*President Adams*), and *Upshur* (ex-*President Hayes*).

'We're glad to have our ship back,' was the official word out of United States Lines' headquarters and, happily, there had been no disruption in her construction timetable. At the shipyard, some 2,500 men were employed on the *United States* project. There were also several hundred employed elsewhere on various parts of the ship's creation. Apart from the physical construction of the liner, there was the mind-boggling process of producing required items that would go into her: 125,000 pieces of chinaware, 6,000 crystal goblets, 7,000 bedspreads, 4,000 passenger blankets, 44,000 bed sheets, 81,000 face towels, 44,000 pillow slips, and 7 caskets for the hospital. Overall, in the design, there were over 8,000 drawings from which a total of 1,200,000 blueprints were made.

As construction continued at a brisk and unbroken pace, the tonnage estimate jumped yet again, this time to 51,000. This was, of course, under the British standard and was a fair method as almost all other big liners used the same standard. (Under American measurements, she was only a mere 39,900 tons.) It was also made official that the stacks would be the largest of their day—55 ft in height for the forward funnel alone! Otherwise, all else seemed on schedule. The official naming of the ship would take place on Saturday, 23 June 1951.

Almost everyone wanted Bess Truman, the wife of the American President, to christen the *United States*. After all, Mrs Roosevelt had done the honours for the *America* in August 1939. It seemed only fitting to have the next First Lady. An invitation was sent to the White House, but three weeks before the ceremony, on 1 June it was politely declined. A day later, the United States Lines announced that Mrs Tom Connally, the wife of the then well-known Texas senator, would do the honours. The ship, as the publicity reports read, would be 70 per cent complete on the day of 'launching'. One reporter visited the ship at this busy and anxious time, and wrote: 'You go aboard but you don't stay long, because your ears just can't take much of the deafening thunder set off by the riveters, who swarm over every deck. You take a quick tour and see hundreds of men—electricians, welders, shipfitters, pipefitters and all the

Opposite Her sleek, slender, and very long hull form are especially evident in this view, taken on 10 June 1952. (*Newport News Shipbuilding & Dry Dock Co*)

SS United States

Three views of the highly secret engine room. There were no engine room tours aboard the *United States* — the area was off-limits to all passengers and visitors alike. The veil of top secrecy was not lifted on this and other features until as late as 1968. (*United States Lines*)

other craftsmen—helping to build the biggest ship in America's history. And this is the ballroom, your escort-guide tells you above the ear-killing noise, pointing to a big, bare enclosure. But instead of strapless gowns, you see three men in sweat-stained overalls, each one driving rivets like mad.'

Still under the tightest veil of secrecy, and with the military provisions in her design as well, of course, as her actual power and true speed potential closely guarded, there were some public reports about her extraordinary safety features. Indeed, she would be the safest liner ever built. Perhaps the best-known—and enduring—story involves the wood on the *United States*. While there was some aboard the older *America*, there was absolutely none in the new superliner— except in the butcher's block and the piano. Earlier, it seems that William Francis Gibbs and Theodore Steinway, the world famous piano maker, had 'very strained' discussions about a possible aluminium piano. Gibbs lost the battle (one of the very few). There were also jokes such as, 'Gibbs has even insisted on an aluminium baton for the orchestra leader, but we ask: Are the musicians fireproof?'.

There was also great curiosity about the ship's two duplicate engine rooms. Spaced well apart, they were among the most important of the Defense Department's ingredients in her design and potential as a wartime trooper. It gave the liner a special invulnerability as a troopship. Even if one torpedo hit and incapacitated one engine room, the other could be utilized to maintain adequate steam and power. Of course, this had been done before, towards the end of the

Second World War, with the P2-type troopships. They, too, had costly double engine rooms. After the war, however, when it was planned to sail many of these ex-military ships as commercial liners, this feature proved a great handicap. Two engine rooms meant additional staff and expense. Consequently, only one of them, the converted *La Guardia* (mentioned in more detail in Chapter 2) was never a success as a passenger vessel. But in the buoyantly optimistic mood that surrounded the construction of the *United States*, operating expenses seemed not to matter. Her success was assured—almost at any cost—and even when the actual amount had sky-rocketed to $78 million. This was an added distinction: she was the most expensive merchant ship of all time.

The 'launching' process would take 53 hours and 41 minutes prior to her actual christening. Being built in a graving dock, the ship was not, of course, able to be launched in the more traditional way. Instead, the dock would be gradually flooded and then the ship floated. In a very detailed, minute-by-minute schedule, the liner would be fully afloat at just after five in the morning on the christening day.

It all went like clockwork. There was no wind at all; the 'big ship' was named, and then gently moved out of her building berth to the north side of the shipyard's Pier 10 for final outfitting. She looked splendid. But long after Mrs Connally and the other distinguished guests had departed from the special naming platform, and after thousands of other guests in the yard had left as well, there was still one rather mystifying oddity: there had been no place on the main platform for William Francis Gibbs, the genius creator of the genius ship. Instead he watched the ceremonies from the sidelines.

Life magazine called the liner 'a proud present for the Nation on her 175th anniversary of independence'. Excitement—and expectation—reached an even higher pitch. Less than a week after the naming, and when the question of her top speed was still a mystery, the first of several optimistic headlines read: 'SUPERLINER AIMS AT ATLANTIC RECORD'. Within official ranks, however, there were also all sorts of speculation, even some caution. Gibbs himself warned that no attempt at a record run at maximum speed should be made for some time, or at least until the crew were fully familiar with the ship. Furthermore, there was talk that the United States Lines ought to improve gradually on existing records, but only by a few minutes each year in order to gain continual publicity and notoriety. Across the Atlan-

tic, there were other rumours as well, all of them concerned with the speed record. The most common was that the *Queen Elizabeth* would finally show her true paces and outstep even her record-breaking mate, the *Queen Mary*. The *Elizabeth*, which was completed four years after the *Mary*, in 1940, was never 'pushed' to her maximum speed—or at least to an officially recorded speed that would have broken the existing record. In retrospect, several senior Cunard officers added that it was simply too expensive, even foolish, to 'push' the *Elizabeth* at such an enormous speed. After all, there was no sense in taking the Penant from one of your own ships. Even more realistically, it would have been most unlikely that the *Elizabeth* could have outpaced the new American superliner. The second rumour stemming from Britain was that Cunard would build a new supership of their own as soon as the American liner was in service. This was perhaps even less likely, especially in the early and mid 1950s. It was far too soon to replace either of the existing *Queens*, and then, of course, such a new giant would be something of an odd man out. Additionally, neither of these rumours quite fit-

The first arrival at New York, in the Lower Bay and surrounded by her welcoming flotilla of tugs. (*United States Lines*)

The *United States* passes the Battery, the tip of Manhattan island, and the United States Lines headquarters as well as the Gibbs & Cox offices. (*United States Lines*)

ted with Cunard's official position on the speed record and the Blue Riband. The Liverpool headquarters re-stated that record-breaking speed was not a priority, but that reliability, safety, and passenger comfort were far more important. The *Queens*, so they said, were built for speed simply to cope with the creation of a two- rather than a three-ship express run.

Another small oddity of the time was that the Hales Trophy, that special gilded creation that customarily went to Blue Riband liners, was missing. It had been made by the late Harold Keates Hales, a former Member of Parliament, and had been last accepted by the French Line, in 1935, for record passages by their magnificent *Normandie*. When the *Queen Mary* snatched the Penant in 1938, however, Cunard refused it, using the claim that they were not so interested in record speeds. And so the trophy went back to its donor and then, quite unknown to almost everyone else, to the silversmith who made it. In fact, it was 'missing' for over a decade before a search was mounted. Some even suspected that it had never left the *Normandie* and had been burned with her in her New York berth, in February 1942. The search finally led, in August 1951, to the rediscovery of the trophy. It would, of course, eventually go to the Americans and then come to the United States, where it has remained ever since.

Serious training courses for staff members on the *United States* began in September 1951. 'At Newport News, I lived in a little hotel,' recalled David Fitzgerald, then acting as an assistant purser, but who years later would become chief purser of the superliner. 'We did our training ashore, in mock-ups of staterooms. We had to learn thoroughly deck plans and almost all passenger aspects of the ship. There were also deck officers and engineers with us.' A month later, the first advertising for the *United States* appeared. Reservations were being accepted! These first promotional pieces included a well-known reproduction of a painting of the ship—one that had slightly smaller funnels (and a pair more like those on the *America*) and a mainmast (again, almost exactly like the *America*). The funnels on the new liner were, of course, to be larger and the mainmast never went aboard (it was almost certainly never intended).

The maiden voyage was now set for 3 July, and passage rates would begin at $360 in first class, $230 in cabin class, and $170 in tourist class. The top suites went for $930.

By New Year 1951-2, with the *America* at the shipyard for her annual overhaul, the two liners were side by side and, more clearly than ever, the general similarities in design could be seen. Clearly, the *America* had led to the bigger *United States*. That same month, and with the larger liner now 85 per cent complete, the force at the shipyard had climbed to 3,100, surely making it the largest peacetime project at Newport News.

In that busy final winter and spring of construction there were two other news items. On 11 March a gale blew the Panamanian-flag freighter *Shakin* into the pristine stern of the *United States*, though luckily only slight damage resulted. The other item was another of those curious oddities, another rumour, in which the United States and Britain were supposed to have agreed that the new liner would operate at a speed less than that of either of the two Cunard *Queens*. It was said that the *United States* would use a service speed of less than 28 knots (the *Queens* maintained averages of 28½ knots). In actuality, the new American giant would have an average service speed of 32-3 knots, which was even higher than the *Mary's* 1938 Blue Riband record of 31.69 knots.

The first trials began on 14 May, with the ship just slightly more than 90 per cent complete. The results were extremely favourable and certainly most encouraging. The three major facts derived from this trial run were: it was now without question that this liner would make the speed record; that she was noticeably free of vibrations, even in high winds and rough seas; and that she would be an excellent seaboat, even a comfortable riding ship. Historically, the last American-flag passenger ship to win the Blue Riband had been exactly a century before. The Collins Line's *Baltic* made a record crossing of 9 days and 13 hours, at an average speed of 13.34 knots. Now the goal—still a close secret—was under 4 days at about 35 knots average.

The second and more official series of trials began on 9 June, and this time 1,700 invited guests, reporters and part of her crew (1,036 would be the exact number once she was in service) were on board. Her actual gross tonnage was finally released and placed at 53,290, over 5,000 tons more than those first estimates. On this short voyage there were crash stops, full rudder tests, stability tests, even a stint spent travelling in reverse—and at 20 knots! But the big news was her maximum speed—would it exceed the *Queen Mary*'s record? The official word was limited to 'in excess of 34 knots', surely faster than the *Mary*, but then nowhere near her actual maximum capability. A few select guests were given the amazing news, however. She reached an astonishing 39.38 knots. This meant an extraordinary total shaft horsepower of 241,785—and what a record when compared to the 158,000 maximum of each of the *Queens*!

'The trials were run entirely by the shipbuilders,' remembered David Fitzgerald, who was aboard. 'The United States Lines people were technically "guests". There were 150 of us [United States Lines] people in all, and it was out deck crews that were running her. We raced up and down the Virginia Capes, and did all sorts of mechanical tests. The absolute top secret was that she did an incredible 43 knots for a short time and even outpaced a speeding Navy destroyer. The *United States* behaved like a Chris Craft.'

The *United States* was handed over officially by the government to the United States Lines on 20 June, in a rather simple ceremony in an office in Hoboken, New Jersey. The ship was, of course, delivered on the same day, at Newport News. 'When Commodore Harry Manning took delivery of the ship,' recalled his eventual successor, Captain and later Commodore Alexanderson, 'the shipyards presented him with a very elaborate shortwave radio. But it had a wooden case. Gibbs saw it and removed it at once. He replaced it with a similar model, but with a metal case. Everything had to be fireproof. Not even wood in the picture frames were allowed. If he found wood in frames, he would take the frames down and take the picture to his New York office.

They would be returned, but with aluminium frames.'

Two days later, on the 22nd, she took on more invited guests (this time, there were 1,200 in all) for the overnight run up to New York and her first gala reception. There were 162 reporters, but only two women (both crewmembers). She arrived in New York harbour and received what at least one veteran tugboat captain termed 'The greatest reception I can remember.' Surrounded by tugs and launches, fireboats, and specially chartered excursion craft—and with small planes and helicopters overhead—she passed the Battery, the United States Lines headquarters at 1 Broadway, and the Gibbs & Cox offices at nearby 21 West Street just after midday. Whistles, horns, and sirens were sounding everywhere—and, of course, those mighty steam whistles, said to be the most powerful afloat, responded to the welcoming salutes. 'Welcome' signs were hung from office windows, and all American-flag ships berthed along the Hudson waterfront were dressed in flags for the occasion.

Not everyone witnessed the reception. 'I was below deck, busy with a million details,' recalled David Fitzgerald. 'It was a tremendous job preparing the *United States*. It seemed as if we worked a full 24 hours every day and for weeks!'

The 'Big Ship' is eased, for the very first time, into a berth at Pier 86, at the foot of West 46th Street. (*United States Lines*)

Chapter 4

Crossings and Cruises

Over 123,000 lb of meat were placed aboard the *United States* for her maiden crossing, set to begin on 3 July 1952. There would also be some 60,000 lb of poultry and 12,000 quarts of milk. Over 1,700 passengers would make the first trip, including Margaret Truman, the daughter of the President, and William Francis Gibbs himself. A special maiden voyage booklet was thoughtfully printed. She departed from the north berth of Pier 86 precisely at noon and, little more than 2½ hours later, at 2:36, passed the Ambrose Light. This was the traditional starting point for all east-bound attempts at the Blue Riband — that is, of course, if there *was* to be a serious attempt. The ship's clocks were adjusted.

Within the first two days, the ship averaged an amazing 35 knots. Soon after, she was reported to be passing over the 36-knot mark. The Riband was assured—she would break the *Queen Mary*'s record by six, and possibly as much as ten, hours! Waves and cheers and whistle salutes were received en route from, among others, the French Line's *Liberté*, herself a former Blue Riband champion, when sailing in the early 1930s as Germany's *Europa*. A cordial telegram was received from the master of the *Queen Mary*, and later the two big liners passed one another, and at full speed no less. The *Queen Elizabeth*'s captain, already aware of the imminent victory by the new American, commented somewhat reluctantly, 'You can take it for granted that there will be no attempt [by Cunard] to beat the *United States.*'

Officially, the *United States* captured the Blue Riband, on Monday, 7 July at precisely 5.16 am GMT. She made the crossing in 3 days, 10 hours and 40 minutes, at an average speed of 35.59 knots. This was 3.9 knots faster than the *Mary*'s record from 1938. The whistles were sounded and cheers broke out throughout the ship. The band began to play, even despite the early hour, and some passengers, who had been awake all night, started a festive conga line. The ship seemed to be celebrating from stem to stern.

Marjorie Marshall, who would later become the liner's senior telephone switchboard operater, was aboard for this historic maiden trip:

I arrived at 8 in the morning, on the 3rd, for that first sailing. The previous days had been full of parties and receptions and tours for the public, but this day the pier was especially bustling. There was baggage and banners and bands. The ship was filled. It seemed to be bursting. It was difficult to find one's way around. Four of us were assigned to the two telephone rooms on the Main Deck. We sailed exactly at noon. Briefly, I walked through the crowds. It was awesome, exciting, everyone was breathless with anticipation. Actually, I was on duty at the very moment we sailed away from Pier 86, but all of us could hear the huge clatter.

The first afternoon, the switchboard was ablaze. Mostly, there were calls asking directions about the ship and two of us used a mounted deck-plan set before us. I was off-duty by 4. The ship had quietened-down, but there was still a sense of hub-bub. I felt a sense of happy exhaustion. The next day, there were more calls,

3 July 1952: the *United States* begins what will be her triumphant, record breaking maiden eastbound run. The cruiseship *Nassau* is just to the left; the *Excambion* of American Export berthed across the Hudson in Jersey City. (*Moran Towing & Transportation Co*)

Souvenir log cards
from the eastbound
and westbound
maiden voyages.

MAIDEN VOYAGE
QUADRUPLE SCREW TURBINE STEAMSHIP
"UNITED STATES"
COMMODORE HARRY MANNING
Captain, U.S.N.R.

Abstract of Log   Voyage 1, Eastbound
From NEW YORK to SOUTHAMPTON via LE HAVRE

DATE	LAT. N	LONG.W	NAUT. MILES	SPEED	WIND	REMARKS
July 3						Departure Ambrose L.V., 2:36 p.m., E.D.T.
July 4	41-12	58-43	696	34.11	SW-4	Slight Sea
July 5	45-03	41-42	801	35.60	SW-4	Moderate Sea
July 6	49-04	22-41	814	36.17	Var-5	Moderate Sea
July 7	49-49	01-14	833	36.21	Var-5	Bishop Rock Abeam, 6:16 a.m., B.S.T.
July 7			47		Var-5	Arrived Havre L.V., 1:24 p.m., B.S.T.

Passage, AMBROSE L.V. to BISHOP ROCK: 2,942 Miles
3 Days, 10 Hours, 40 Minutes — Average Speed: 35.59 Knots

Total Distance, NEW YORK to LE HAVRE: 3,191 Miles
Steaming Time: 3 Days, 17 Hours, 48 Minutes — Average Speed: 35.53 Knots

NOTE: A Nautical Mile is approximately 15 percent longer than a Statute or Land Mile

These passages are world records. It is the first time in a century that an American ship has captured the Blue Ribbon of the North Atlantic. The United States Lines is rightfully proud of the achievement. We believe you are too.

Left Havre L.V., 12:46 p.m., B.S.T., July 8, 1952   Arrived Nab Tower, 3:37 p.m., B.S.T., July 8, 1952
Distance, LE HAVRE L.V. to NAB TOWER: 75 Miles
Steaming Time: 2 Hours, 51 Minutes — Average Speed: 26.31 Knots

MAIDEN VOYAGE
QUADRUPLE SCREW TURBINE STEAMSHIP
"UNITED STATES"
COMMODORE HARRY MANNING
Captain, U.S.N.R.

Abstract of Log   Voyage 1, Westbound
From SOUTHAMPTON to NEW YORK via LE HAVRE

Left Nab Tower, 5:00 p.m., B.S.T., July 10, 1952   Arrived Havre L.V., 7:24 p.m., B.S.T., July 10, 1952
Distance, NAB TOWER to LE HAVRE L.V.: 75 Miles
Steaming Time: 2 Hours, 24 Minutes — Average Speed: 31.25 Knots

DATE	LAT. N	LONG.W	NAUT. MILES	SPEED	WIND	REMARKS
July 11						Departure Havre L.V., 2:00 a.m., B.S.T.
July 11	49-49	08-49	341	34.10	W-5	Abeam Bishop Rock, 9:17 a.m., B.S.T.
July 12	48-10	31-35	902	36.08	W-3	Moderate Sea
July 13	42-56	50-43	865	33.92	Var-2	Light Fog; Speed Reduced
July 14	40-26	69-51	872	34.19	Var-1	Smooth Sea, Hazy
July 14			175			Arrived Ambrose L.V., 4:29 p.m., E.D.T.

Passage, BISHOP ROCK to AMBROSE L.V.: 2,906 Miles
3 Days, 12 Hours, 12 Minutes — Average Speed: 34.51 Knots

Total Distance, LE HAVRE to NEW YORK: 3,155 Miles
Steaming Time: 3 Days, 19 Hours, 29 Minutes — Average Speed: 34.48 Knots

NOTE: A Nautical Mile is approximately 15 percent longer than a Statute or Land Mile

These passages are world records. It is the first time in a century that an American ship has captured the Blue Ribbon of the North Atlantic both East and West passages. The United States Lines is rightfully proud of the achievement. We believe you are too.

from both passengers and crew alike. Margaret Truman was just across the corridor [in Cabin M66] and had 24-hour guards. She was very thoughtful and gave the phone operators two large vases of roses.

The passengers became more and more breathless with excitement. They were constantly betting in the Main Lounge on whether or not the ship would take the Riband. There were endless calls to us asking about the mileage. It was a make-believe voyage. In other ways, there were the regular activities: films, bingo, teas.

Finally, on the third day, we reached Bishop's Rock. We broke the record! We had the Blue Riband! How exciting! We cried with excitement and pride. As we went up the Solent to Southampton, the whistles seemed never to cease. The shouting was overwhelming as we arrived. There was hugging and kissing and more tears. There was a huge escort in the Solent and many of the boats looked overloaded. Many of them seemed to be waving American flags.

We remained in Southampton for several days. There was a big open house, tours and visits by dignitaries. Afterward, we went across to Le Havre. We wouldn't go to Bremerhaven for the first time until fall. There was also a gala, very friendly French reception.

The weather was ideal for the roundtrip, being July. We had smooth sailing both ways. Many of the passengers made the roundtrip with us and then we were met at New York by President and Mrs Truman. There was huge fanfare and triumph at New York, and another joyous reception. The President came aboard and received his daughter in the Main Lounge. Milton Berle and Vincent Astor also sailed home with us. The docking took quite long at Pier 86, since it was only the second time since the ship's delivery. The orchestra was continuously playing the 'Star Spangled Banner'. Everyone was crying, including Margaret Truman and Milton Berle. What glory!

The *United States* received an enormous reception at Southampton, greater even that at New York, and certainly greater than at Le Havre. Some went so far as to state that the Southampton reception was the greatest given to a ship anywhere at any time. Even the Prime Minister, Winston Churchill, sent greetings and congratulations. High enthusiasm prevailed and there were news reports, prompted by the general euphoria, predicting that 'the

A striking view of the outbound liner, also in July 1952, but from the windows of Gibbs & Cox at 21 West Street. (*United States Lines*)

United States will be the world's foremost liner for the next fifty years!'

She returned home, sailing westbound with just over 1,600 passengers, on 10 July. She reached Ambrose Light on the 14th. Again, there was a record—3 days, 12 hours, 12 minutes, at 34.51 knots. Among other well-known songs, the band began to play 'I'm Just Wild About Harry', in fond tribute to the ship's master, Commodore Harry Manning. Once at New York, the liner flew the 40-ft banner of the Blue Riband and gave no fewer than 400 whistle salutes to other ships in the harbour. A ticker-tape parade up Lower Broadway was organized.

Of course, there was widespread speculation that the liner would go on to break her own records. William Francis Gibbs would never deny that a 40-knot speed was possible, though the ship's chief engineer was more cautious: 'Simply, there was no reason for the liner to break her own record—and then, quite practically, there is the question of the great expense of it all.'

The *United States* carried a record 36,044 passengers in her first Atlantic season. This was well over 90 per cent occupancy and the United States Lines were more than satisfied. She would remain the most popular and profitable single superliner on the North Atlantic for the next decade or so. The flagship of the entire US merchant fleet, the largest liner ever built in America, and, of course, the Blue Riband all contributed to making the *United States* a very special ship. But there were other reasons as well for her great popularity and initial success.

'She was not as stuffy as the big British liners,' felt David Fitzgerald. 'She was more friendly—and there was more conversation with the staff. The physical layout was also excellent. Almost from the start, she had a huge reputation and, of course, there was her great speed. Generally, she was a happy, well working ship. By comparison, the *America* was a dim, little liner. On the *United States*, it was brighter and shinier and crisper.

'Many passengers took her out of a patriotic spirit. Many felt that they would be better understood on an American ship. The first- and cabin-class sections were extremely well run. The maintenance and care of the ship was also meticulous.

'Of course, the passengers were quite different in those years. Transatlantic passengers had more class, more purpose in their travels. There were also many, many loyalist passengers, people who went over to Europe every June and then returned in August or September. There were people

who made six roundtrips in six years! Every sailing, and especially in later years, was like old home week. I'd always check the passenger lists and always knew at least a few names.'

Commodore Alexanderson felt that she was one of the best maintained ships anywhere and that this contributed greatly to her very special appeal. 'Perhaps, she was even the cleanest ship anywhere. Even the engine room was always in fantastic condition. She also had excellent food and great variety in her menus. There were some cost cuts toward the end of her life, but the *United States* was never tatty.'

'Cleanliness was always a huge factor,' added Al Grant, one of the ship's assistant pursers. 'The passengers always used to comment on the lack, for example, of a ship's smell—an odour that pervaded almost all other liners, including the *Queens*. Physically, the *United States* had great majesty. She had an extraordinary exterior. You always felt you were in the presence of a real ocean queen.

'She was also the safest ship afloat. The safety requirements were exceptional. But we never, ever said "unsinkable". Personally, I liked the decor as well [generally, it was often criticized as being too severe, almost austere], mostly because it was like a ship, not some recreation of a moun-

The glorious return: the newest Blue Riband champion. Note the pennant attached to the radar mast atop the wheelhouse. (*United States Lines*)

109

SS United States

tain lodge. She was unmistakably American.

'The food was also great. Americans often didn't understand European cuisine and so they were far more comfortable with American food. Many wealthy passengers, for example, didn't they know what they were ordering on the gourmet French liners. We also had lots of Germans in the galley staff and so there were often pleasant German specialities on the menus. Onboard, we gave substantial portions that so typified European impressions of America: abundance.

'The ship was very, very comfortable. She had every creature comfort. Mostly, we had smiling faces at disembarkation. Once, we had an opera singer, who always went on the Italian Line, but there was a strike and so he took the *United States*. He remained with us for years and once told me, "I can't believe what I've been missing by not sailing on the *United States*".'

'She was so beautiful and so comfortable,' added senior telephonist Marjorie Marshall, 'and for the passengers as well as the crew. The food was also superb, but I feel that there was a great specialness in her being American. We were all very proud to have such a superb ship running on the Atlantic. In the early years, the service was impeccable,

Far left The first-class dining-room was two decks high and done in oyster white walls. The chairs were light red. (*Frank O. Braynard Collection*)

Below far left The private first-class restaurant, used by the Windsors and other noted passengers. (*Frank O. Braynard Collection*)

Below A superb first-class cabin. (*Frank O. Braynard Collection*)

Leisurely long
afternoons aboard the
world's fastest ship.
(*George Devol
Collection*)

but in later years, with the sale of the United States Lines
to the Walter Kidde Co, the once sterling standards lessened.
The priorities changed.'

The *United States* carried a full crew of 1,036. 'When new,
50 per cent of the crew came from the *America*', recalled David
Fitzgerald, 'and 50 per cent were just hired. Stewards and
waiters generally want the newest ships. They are more
popular, carry more passengers and so there are better
chances of more tips. Tourist class was the exception, of
course. We tended to carry more budget people in those
quarters. Actually, cabin class often had rich and sometimes
very rich passengers, but who didn't want to pay first-class
fares. In cabin class, we also had lots of substantial Washington, DC types and also people who didn't want to bring their
evening clothes along.'

The *United States* made continuous runs between New
York, Le Havre, and Southampton, and had occasional
extensions up to Bremerhaven. The *America* did the same,
although on an independent schedule, and also included
Cobh in Ireland. 'The passengers were usually evenly
divided between Southampton and Le Havre,' recalled Al
Grant. 'Bremerhaven was more variable—more seasonal and
more dependent on the US military flow. The senior military officers, the majors and up, tended to go in first class.
The enlisted and junior grades, and often with their families, went in cabin class.'

'On her regular crossings, we'd average 32 knots,' according to Commodore Alexanderson. 'We'd use six out of the
eight boilers. We'd start out at New York at 32 knots, but then

ease down by the time we reached the English Channel.

'We thought of the crossings as 4 days, 8 hours,' added the Commodore. 'I'd go down to the dining-room on the second, third, and possibly the fourth nights. On the second night, we'd have the Commodore's cocktail party for about 35 passengers. On transatlantic crossings, I'd have the same guests at my table throughout the voyage, but on cruises we'd invite different guests each night.'

The *United States* usually sailed at noon, from Pier 86, along New York's 'Luxury Liner Row'. Those mighty whistles would sound, echoing along that part of the waterfront and even into the city itself, to signal her departure. 'There were three whistles—two in the forward stack and one in the aft stack', according to the Commodore. 'Sometimes, we would sound two together or combine all three. It varied. These whistles had been special projects of Mr Gibbs and he wanted an exact tone. Before the ship was commissioned, he had the sound tested in the Jersey Meadows, just west of New York City. When the ship was later retired by the Maritime Administration [1973], the whistles were removed and placed in the holds. The stack openings were covered. Now [1989], she has no voice. How amazing!'

'On sailing day at New York,' added Captain Robert Brooks, 'we always had a special aft propeller watch posted. In the Hudson, in those busy days, we always had to check for other craft.'

'The *United States* was a crackerjack operationally,' recalled Chief Purser Fitzgerald. 'She was extremely efficient and performed well even in rough weather, although she tended

'The route of the unrushables' — a quiet corner on the *Big U*. (*George Devol Collection*)

SS United States

Gala dining in the
first-class restaurant.
(*Alexanderson Collection*)

After-dinner dancing
in the Main Ballroom.
(*Alexanderson Collection*)

The captain's table —
eastbound, April 1961.
(*Alexanderson Collection*)

Captain's Reception — Captain (later Commodore) Alexanderson is to the right of centre; Mrs William Dougherty (later Mrs Alexanderson) is third from the left. The date is March 1964. (*Alexanderson Collection*)

The 'captain's tiger' — Pete Thomopoulos. (*Alexanderson Collection*)

to roll. I remember one storm, with a 16-18° roll, when it seemed that a bottle of Scotch was pouring *up* my sleeve!'

In a letter to the author in November 1987, Brooke (Mrs Vincent) Astor wrote, 'Once aboard the *United States*, the *Queen Elizabeth* was trying to catch up with us. Captain Astor [Vincent, a board member of the United States Lines] jumped up from the luncheon table, when informed of this fact, and dashed up to the bridge. He arranged that the *United States* should "kick up her heels" and dash at a terrific pace across the sea. The passengers, not quite understanding what was happening, were in a panic for a while, but soon entered into the fun and were particularly pleased. We arrived at New York seven hours ahead of time!'

Leslie Barton was the chief quartermaster and recalled, 'Operationally, the *Big U* was like a young colt. You couldn't fight her. You always had to anticipate her. She was skittish, light and was always her own boss—but she would listen to reason. Somehow, she sensed if you knew what you were doing. As examples, you could never give her more than 20° rudder and 35° hard over. At full speed, it would be eight miles before she could be stopped.

'The *United States* "yawed" in foul weather. Her stacks especially were like big sails. Yet she was only late four times in 400 trips. The longest was a 12-hour delay. The others were less, usually getting into New York by afternoon rather than the customary 8 am docking.

'The *United States* was light and therefore rode like a duck. She rolled with the waves. Comparatively, she handled very well. The *Queens* were too heavy and tended to drop down quickly. Sea waves come in threes, then there's a valley. The *Big U* would pound whereas the *Queens* would drop. The big *Majestic* once dropped so badly that her forward decking was cracked. The bow on the *Big U* was like a razor, a very sharp razor, while her stern section tended to slide, which we called "yawing." In bad weather, we'd usually reduce speed to about 20 knots.'

Leslie Barton also recalled an incident on one crossing when a passenger jumped overboard. 'On the bridge, we immediately started the Williamson turn, which meant that we'd turn the ship in the same direction as the man who jumped so as to avoid the suction of the stern. She kept moving as she was swinging to starboard [right]. She then made a 180°–turn, and we returned to lower the boats. Below, she was shaking and straining. The *United States* always had stern vibration, especially in a so-called following sea or following wind. She would lift in the stern and her props would not grab as much. Sometimes, usually with other quartermasters, she would "get away" from them. She would swing off course. Once you tried to rectify this, she'd begin to "yaw". The *United States* was a very sensitive ship, but she responded very quickly.'

The younger passengers!
(*Alexanderson Collection*)

Above Commodore Alexanderson. (*Alexanderson Collection*)

Above right High above the Hudson, on the port bridge wing, Captain Alexanderson surveys his outbound ship. (*Alexanderson Collection*)

Opposite Another fine view of Captain Alexanderson, with the ship's trim silver-painted radar mast behind him. (*Alexanderson Collection*)

'It was tense all the time,' recalled Mr Barton. 'There were split second decisions all the time. Sleep was often intermittent. In port, we'd close the bridge and then soon reopen it for sailing. I'd get the flags out and always check to be sure that they were in perfect condition. Everything had to be exact.'

Barton had had considerable experience with passenger ships. He began, in 1934, as a dishwasher on the old *Leviathan*. 'I earned $28 a month and brought my own knife and fork, plate and straw mattress bed.' Afterward, he served in the *President Roosevelt* of United States Lines and then in the affiliate Panama Pacific Line's *California* and *Pennsylvania*. After the Second World War, he rejoined the former *California* in her new career as Moore McCormack Lines' *Uruguay* until he rejoined the United States Lines in the mid 1950s. He later became chief quartermaster of the fastest liner in the world. 'After that last trip, from New York to Newport News, in November 1969, I was the last person to ring-up "finished with engines". She never sailed again and thereafter was "dead". I called down to the junior engineer in the engine room at 7.15 that morning [8 November]. I didn't fully realize, however, that it was the very last time.'

Some of the worst moments for Quartermaster Barton

were those odd and often very risky times when the *United States* had to dock herself as a result of New York harbour tugs being on strike:

Normally, the docking took 35-45 minutes, but at those times it took 2¼ hours. There was also one enormous hurricane in the North Atlantic when we lost the floodlights on the forward king-posts, several bridge windows were cracked and waves continuously poured over the bow. Also, sometimes going along the Weser River [at Bremerhaven] could be very risky. An easterly wind would make the *Big U* slide. There wasn't much water in the river so we were worried about her touching. Only once, however, in a very thick fog, we anchored off and waited out the night.

Also, during a Caribbean cruise, at Kingston, Jamaica, we bent a propeller blade during a difficult manoeuvre. A little local tug tried to help and her captain later remarked, 'Sometimes a mouse can help a lion!' The blade was later straightened by divers at Pier 86. On another occasion, during our South Atlantic cruise, we put into Port Elizabeth in South Africa. We had been to Capetown and landed passengers that wanted to go overland on a safari and so we were due to return there to retrieve them. At Port Elizabeth,

there was a rather poor tug service in that smallish harbour. Suddenly, a 'southerner' came up from the Antarctic region. The *Big U* was broadside to the wind and just held. Those stacks were like sails. We just couldn't get away from the dock. The sailing had to be postponed until that evening. Later, while rounding the

Cape of Good Hope, and being followed by a South African Air Force fighter plane, the pilot above radioed to us and asked our speed. He couldn't believe it was 40 knots. We were sailing onwards to Luanda in Angola. Someone else recalled 41 knots, but I can't seem to verify this!

Once, the United States Lines was sued for an old lady's lunch. We were going up the Solent, using a 'choice pilot', which meant he was selected and we didn't go in rotation. Usually, it was three hours up to our berth. Half way up, at Calshot Spit, we had to complete a 180°-turn. Once, a woman was sitting on the sandy shore there and eating her lunch. The *Big U* caused a 'wash' and her lunch was taken into the sea. She later sued for £5 and won her case. The United States Lines actually loved the publicity. But thereafter, the *United States* was told to 'watch her wash!'

Commodore Leroy Alexanderson had been assigned to the *United States* as executive officer and relieving master in September 1955. He would arrive on the bridge four hours before the liner's noontime sailings from New York. Among other details, he would receive a VIP list of 'preferred passengers', a list that not only included names, titles, and cabin numbers, but home office notations as well. It allowed for the extra, more familiar touches, especially useful in subsequent conversations at a cocktail party, in the dining-room, or on

A wintery arrival at Bremerhaven. (*Al Grant Collection*)

a reception line. 'Of course, however, not all celebrities were on the "Who's Who" list. Some just wanted a quiet, anonymous voyage. Mr Gautier, our vice-president in charge of passenger traffic, would come aboard at 9.30 on sailing day and would discuss, among other details, the special table arrangements to be made with the Chief Steward. The more regular passengers had preferences. The Commodore, the Chief Engineer, Executive Officer, the Doctor and the Chief Purser all had their own tables. When the weather was bad, I would not go down to dinner and, as was the custom, my chair would be left empty.

'On every arrival of the ship, Mr Gibbs would drive in his limousine to Shore Parkway in Brooklyn, quite near the Verrazano Bridge, and watch the *United States* arrive. His chauffeur would then take off for Pier 86 and Gibbs would observe the docking and her final arrival, which was usually at about 7 or 7.15. Afterward, he'd come aboard and go directly to the captain's quarters and then later to see the Chief Engineer. Oddly, I don't seem to recall him ever using a notebook. It seemed to be all mental. On sailing days, it was all done in reverse. He'd come aboard prior to departure, ask more questions, see me and then the Chief Engineer. He would then leave and drive downtown to his offices at 21 West Street and watch the ship sail past.'

Cruising in the swingin' sixties: the *United States* dressed in flags and anchored off Charlotte Amalie, St Thomas.
(*Alexanderson Collection*)

Framed by a tropical palm tree, the *United States* is serviced by tenders off Nassau. (*Alexanderson Collection*)

Once underway and at sea, big ships like the *United States* were settings for a variety of rather unusual events. 'Of course, we'd come across all sorts of passengers—the rich, the famous and so many others,' recalled the Commodore. 'I remember one very wealthy, but very eccentric woman who took a suite for herself and another first-class cabin for her husband. She used to request caviar in her suite and always prior to sailing. Her daughter always came aboard as a visitor with several small jars. The daughter used to pack up the salt-free European caviar that we used on board, but which did not comply with the Pure Food and Drug Act ashore in the States. Happily, the daughter then carried the jars ashore.

'Sometimes, we'd have unexpected passengers. On one

124

trip, after sailing at noon and with winter snow on the decks, the master-at-arms discovered what appeared to be a hobo [tramp]. It was midnight, and the man wore a long overcoat, carried only a toothbrush and otherwise seemed confused and distraught. He had boarded at New York as a visitor, paying the customary 50c. He was taken to the ship's hospital, given a bath and then a bed. He had no identification. We finally notified the New York office and they did some checking. Gradually, it was discovered that he had come from Cleveland. He had been an engineer for a major firm, but had been missing for several years. He made the roundtrip with us and was later reunited with his family at Pier 86. They were grateful to have found him and paid his roundtrip tourist class fare.

'Another unexpected passenger was also on an outbound trip from New York. We'd sailed at noon, passed the pilot station at 2 pm and then, at about 3, he presented himself and asked to leave with the pilot! It was too late. He reported that he had fallen asleep in his girlfriend's cabin and therefore was without a proper passport or travel clothes. We called our New York office and they contacted his wife to ask for his passport. But once she heard the full story, she refused to help. At Le Havre, he was issued a special permit, but was not allowed to go ashore. Once returned to New York, he had to pay a full roundtrip fare. A year or so later, the same gentleman reappeared but as a passenger. He was now divorced and had remarried—that same girlfriend in the cabin!

Christmas Eve in port: the *United States* at Southampton with a lighted Christmas tree atop her radar mast. (*Alexanderson Collection*)

SS United States

'A surprise passenger,' recalled the Commodore, 'was my grade school teacher Miss Aste. She lived around the corner from my family [in Sheepshead Bay] and I'd once stolen some roses from her garden. My mother made me return them, of course! Years later, and while looking over the passenger list in my quarters, I spotted Miss Aste's name. I invited her to a cocktail party. She arrived and indeed she remembered. We became reacquainted quickly, but then she barked in conclusion, "Leroy, I'll speak with you later!" She was still my teacher!

'We'd also had a robbery on board. We were bound for Le Havre and Southampton when the Crew Purser announced that the crew safe had been robbed. We were unsure of the exact amount, but it was in the area of $40,000. The matter was reported to then Commodore Anderson, who immediately wired a message to our Southampton agents and then to our London office. Two British policemen came aboard at Southampton and travelled with us up to Bremerhaven. There were lots of questioning, but no results. It was still a mystery. When we returned to New York,

Far left The inbound *United States* passes the outbound *America* in Southampton Water, May 1960. (*Alexanderson Collection*)

Below far left Another sailing for Europe: the *Big U* moves out of her West 46th Street berth. (*United States Lines*)

Below John L. Lewis, president of the United Mine Workers Union, seems pensive as the *United States* arrives at Pier 86 in February 1957 without tugs. There was a strike and she was forced to berth herself. (*Alexanderson Collection*)

A dramatic aerial view of Pier 86: the *America* on the left; the *United States* on the right. Sections of the Greek *New York* and then the French *Liberté* can be seen on the right. (*Everett Viez Collection*)

a number of FBI agents came aboard. There were still no clues in the case. Six months later, and as the FBI continued its investigation, it was finally uncovered that a crewmember gained access to the safe's combination and then stole the money. He wrapped it in a raincoat and then went ashore and stashed it in a construction site at Le Havre. Six months later, he attempted to retrieve it, but it was all wet and soggy. Some of it was even mutilated. He tried to "iron" some of it and then tried to pass it off through the cabin-class passenger purser. He was caught and later went to prison.

'There were always "rackets" going on in big liners and the *United States* was no exception,' recalled the Commodore. 'There were loansharks and gambling and card games, and finally the wives began to complain that their crewmember-husbands had no money. The crew, falling into debt, would then turn to loansharks. In the gambling games on board, many crewmembers thought that they would make a fortune. But this was very rarely the case and so many were greeted at Pier 86 by the loansharks and forced to pay. In fact, many crewmembers went home with very little money.'

The Commodore also recalled the man-overboard incident. 'We were westbound, on 26 November 1958, at 8.10 in the morning. The officer of the watch noticed a man pacing on the tourist-class outer deck when he suddenly jumped overboard. An immediate hard right was ordered. We turned. The engines were at full speed astern. An extra lookout was posted. Quartermaster Barton threw a life-ring overboard. I carried my trousers in hand and ran to the bridge. No 4 lifeboat, which was a motor lifeboat, was lowered with crew and Dr Sheedy and was sent to recover the passenger. We could barely see the man. There was a moderate swell. We informed the First Officer in the lifeboat to follow our guidance in locating his position: one blast go to starboard, two blasts to port and three blasts to stern. We sounded the whistle to the position of the man. When they finally got him into the lifeboat, he was dead. After all, we were making 32 knots when he jumped and he fell at a height of 60 feet. His body was brought back aboard. The First Officer later reported that he had never heard our whistles. He could only see the steam out of the stacks. The sound went right

A well-known photo: the outbound *America* passes an inbound *United States*. The perspective of the photo makes the 723-ft long *America* appear larger when compared to the 990-ft *United States*. (*Alexanderson Collection*)

Long and sleek, the *United States* passes the Lower Manhattan skyline. (*Port Authority of New York and New Jersey*)

over them. The most amazing thing about this entire incident is that the *United States* stopped in 9 minutes! This was remarkable. Normally, it took 15-20 minutes to stop. The entire rescue took about 45 minutes. Later, we discovered that the man was 84 years old and had deserted his family some years before. Sadly, though, at New York, his brother refused to accept the body. Instead, a group of his brother's friends paid for his burial.'

The *United States* shuttled back and forth to Europe with great regularity. There were few strikes and therefore few disruptions in those early years. Her berthing plans were arranged for 871 in first class, 508 in cabin class, and 549 in tourist class. In that first glory-filled, triumphant decade she maintained a consistent average of over 90 per cent occupancy and was deemed to be a financial success. She was supremely successful in her role as a commercial passenger ship. Fortunately, she never had to prove herself as a trooper. In October 1962, at the time of the Cuban missile crisis, two other US-flag liners, the Moore McCormack cruiseships *Argentina* and *Brasil*, were put on 'standby' by the Defense Department, but the *United States* was not included. Just shortly before, in 1960-61, the *Big U* faced an emergency of her own: she began, and for the first time, to slip into the red. Her costs began to outstrip her passenger revenues and so, in that increasingly jet-dominated decade on the Atlantic, the US government's operating subsidies were needed more and more—and (by the late 1960s) rather

Opposite An interesting perspective: a line handler aboard a Moran tug awaits the call to assist with the undocking of the *Big U* from Pier 86. (*United States Lines*)

25 September 1956: a record 7,000 passengers arrived at 'Luxury Liner Row' and 235 customs inspectors, almost every available man in the port, was on hand. From bottom to top: *Cristoforo Colombo*, Italian Line; the *America*, and then the *United States*; the freighter *Alsatia*, the liner *Queen Elizabeth*, and finally the *Mauretania*, all Cunarders. (*Alexanderson Collection*)

desperately. In her last years, the *United States* was carrying more passengers than either of the *Queens*. It didn't seem to matter. She was losing more and more money—and then there were more labour problems, especially more of those persistent, schedule-disrupting strikes.

On her regular runs, the *United States* used the Gare Maritime at Le Havre, the Columbus Pier at Bremerhaven, and either the Ocean Terminal or the Western Docks at Southampton. At the British port, her arrivals and departures were linked to one of the great icons of transatlantic liner travel, the once numerous boat trains. 'We'd sail from New York at noon and that same afternoon, we'd begin to set up the boat train,' recalled Al Grant, who as an assistant purser was also manager of the ship's travel office. 'After lunch and then following the customary lifeboat drill, we'd have a short break and then looked over the VIP master list sent by the United States Lines' passenger offices. We'd also begin to plan the blocks of space according to passengers in each class for the train.'

We also handled the Boat Train for Le Havre [to/from Paris], but

Sailing from
Southampton's
Western Docks: the
Big U is assisted by
five tugs while Union
Castle's *Capetown
Castle* and brand new
Windsor Castle are in
the background, still
at berth. The date is
October 1960. A US
Navy carrier is berthed
to the left, visiting on
a goodwill tour.
(Alexanderson Collection)

SS United States

A 1966 telegram from *Queen Mary*'s Capt Treasure Jones, and Commodore Alexanderson's reply.

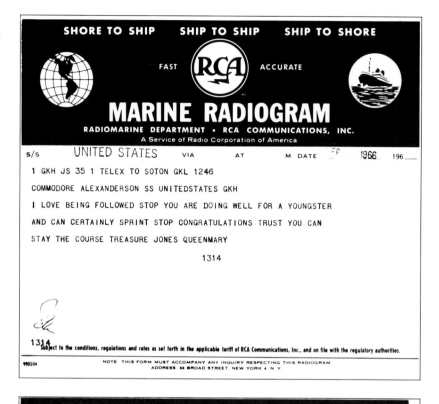

SHORE TO SHIP   SHIP TO SHIP   SHIP TO SHORE

FAST **RCA** ACCURATE

MARINE RADIOGRAM
RADIOMARINE DEPARTMENT • RCA COMMUNICATIONS, INC.
A Service of Radio Corporation of America

s/s   UNITED STATES   VIA   AT   M. DATE   FP   1966   196___

1 GKH JS 35 1 TELEX TO SOTON GKL 1246

COMMODORE ALEXANDERSON SS UNITEDSTATES GKH

I LOVE BEING FOLLOWED STOP YOU ARE DOING WELL FOR A YOUNGSTER

AND CAN CERTAINLY SPRINT STOP CONGRATULATIONS TRUST YOU CAN

STAY THE COURSE TREASURE JONES QUEENMARY

1314

1314 Subject to the conditions, regulations and rates as set forth in the applicable tariff of RCA Communications, Inc., and on file with the regulatory authorities.

995104   NOTE THIS FORM MUST ACCOMPANY ANY INQUIRY RESPECTING THIS RADIOGRAM
ADDRESS 66 BROAD STREET, NEW YORK 4, N Y

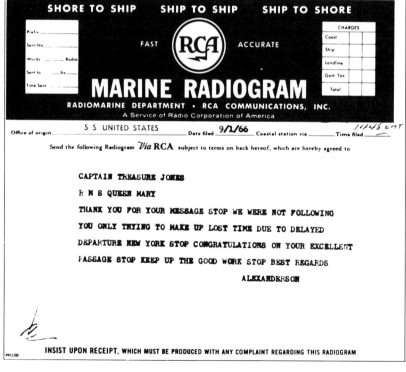

SHORE TO SHIP   SHIP TO SHIP   SHIP TO SHORE

FAST **RCA** ACCURATE

CHARGES
Coast
Ship
Landline
Govt. Tax
Total

MARINE RADIOGRAM
RADIOMARINE DEPARTMENT • RCA COMMUNICATIONS, INC.
A Service of Radio Corporation of America

Office of origin ___ S S UNITED STATES ___ Date filed 9/2/66 Coastal station via ___ Time filed ___

Send the following Radiogram *Via* RCA subject to terms on back hereof, which are hereby agreed to

CAPTAIN TREASURE JONES

R M S QUEEN MARY

THANK YOU FOR YOUR MESSAGE STOP WE WERE NOT FOLLOWING

YOU ONLY TRYING TO MAKE UP LOST TIME DUE TO DELAYED

DEPARTURE NEW YORK STOP CONGRATULATIONS ON YOUR EXCELLENT

PASSAGE STOP KEEP UP THE GOOD WORK STOP BEST REGARDS

ALEXANDERSON

995100   **INSIST UPON RECEIPT, WHICH MUST BE PRODUCED WITH ANY COMPLAINT REGARDING THIS RADIOGRAM**

134

never in Germany. Our Bremen office handled that. In summer, at Southampton, we often needed 10 or 11 British Rail coaches. In fact, 10 or 11 was the maximum length for Waterloo Station's platforms in London. The tourist season was, of course, the busiest. I always booked the train in advance. Passengers usually made their reservations in the first three days of the crossing, but this was not always the case because some of them wanted to wait until the last minute. We'd even send out notice cards to the passengers to encourage them to book. Often, there were sellouts and so some that had waited too long were disappointed.

Some first-class passengers wanted a complete compartment located immediately next to a carriage door. The Windsors, for example, were always given special consideration. Once, we wanted to give actress Irene Pappas a private compartment, but we just couldn't so we thoughtfully joined her with the wife of a United Artists executive. They had much in common and could not have been more pleased. Overall, it was an enormous effort for that 2-3 hour train trip. Someone like Katharine Hepburn would be asked if they wanted to share, but mostly these types of people were travelling with friends or staff. Alternatively the likes of the Eisenhowers would be met by private cars, usually special limousines from American Express.

'The adult fares in the 1960s were $4 in first class [it had climbed to $32 by 1986] and the tickets were stapled onto the passenger reservation cards. The earlier trains took three hours, but later faster trains took about two. I always went up to London for the nights that our trips terminated at Southampton. We usually arrived at 1 or 2 in the afternoon from Le Havre and then the Boat Trains left at about 3 or 4. British customs and immigration had come aboard way out in the Solent, at Calshot, and were very efficient and so were finished by the time we reached the dock. We alternated at Southampton between the Ocean Terminal and the Western Docks. At the Ocean Terminal, however, the *Queens* had priority. On a good summer sailing, as many as 500-600 took the boat train up to London. In addition, there were also car rentals and, of course, passengers staying locally and still others going to different cities, say to Winchester or to Bristol. Some passengers even brought along their own cars, which were carried in the ship's hold. I remember some very fantastic cars, including some great Rolls Royces.

The *United States* had five cargo holds. 'We carried lots of silver bullion from the United States to banks in England,' remembered Captain Robert Brooks. 'There was also lots of first-class, registered and diplomatic mail. We'd have particularly heavy mail loads in the two months prior to Christmas and sometimes so much that it was stowed on the aft open decks. We also carried lots of special and expensive cargos, such as silks and designer clothes. But these items—and along with some of our passengers—started to go by air, in 1960-61.'

The Rich, the Famous and Other Passengers

'They were always very easy to travel with by my standards,' recalled Commodore Alexanderson of that most celebrated couple of post-war transatlantic years, the Duke and Duchess of Windsor. He, the British King who had abdicated in 1936 for 'the woman he loved', and she, the Baltimore divorcee, were, by the 1950s, well established in their luxurious pattern of life: commuting regularly between their homes in Paris and an apartment in New York's Waldorf Towers, as well as winter visits to exclusive Palm Beach in Florida. After the Duke died in 1972 and the Duchess fourteen years later, in 1986, there has been a brisk outpouring of books, as well as magazine and newspaper features, on the fabled couple, their extravagant lifestyle, and, perhaps most poignantly, the loneliness and even purposelessness of it all. Beginning in 1952, the Windsors formed a complete allegiance to the *United States*. Never again would they cross together on another liner. (After the Duke's death, the saddened and very fragile Duchess made at least one more sentimental journey to New York. But with the *United States* by then withdrawn from service, she travelled in and out of Cannes on the French Riviera aboard Italian Line's *Michelangelo*.)

Aboard the *United States*, the Duke, in his polished if slightly eccentric style, and the Duchess, in splendid designer fashions, made indelible impressions on staff and passengers alike. Mostly, the encounters and the remembrances are pleasant and warm. 'They never made any special demands,' recalled Commodore Alexanderson, 'and it was a feather in our cap [United States Lines] to have them. I was never really sure why they selected the *United States*, but they were always treated very well and always occupied the so-called Duck Suite [cabins U87, U89, and U91]. I always had a special chill up my back when the Duke would say, "When I was King...".'

Above The best-known, certainly the most photographed faces in post-war transatlantic liner annals belonged to the Duke and Duchess of Windsor. The famous couple are seen in this view, dated 3 June 1967, while celebrating their 30th wedding anniversary. (*Alexanderson Collection*)

Left Introductions to the senior officers: the Duchess, Commodore Alexanderson, the Duke, Chief Engineer Bill Kaiser, and Captain John Tucker. It was taken on Voyage No 305, westbound, on 2 October 1965. (*Alexanderson Collection*)

```
PARIS  563362 29 4 1730

SEA POST PARIS
S ASSURER SEAPOSTES


PLEASE RELAY TO COMMODORE LEROY ALEXANDERSON SS UNITED STATES
FOLLOWING MESSAGE QUOTE OUR BEST CONGRATULATIONS ON YOUR PROMOTION
STOP WARM REGARDS = DUKE AND DUCHESS OF WINDSOR =

COL SEA POST +

ENVOI 1 +++
SEAPOSTES PARIS
```

Above A telegram to Commodore Alexanderson from the Duke and Duchess. (*Alexanderson Collection*)

The late Kenneth Gautier, vice-president in charge of passenger traffic for United States Lines, reported that 'Despite their overall image, the Windsors lived thriftily. The Duchess was related to General Franklin, the United States Lines' chairman, through her Baltimore relatives and consequently they paid minimum first-class fares only. Quite simply, it was the best deal they had. Cunard wanted them to pay full fare! Another irony, considering that the Duke was very much exiled from his country as well as his family, and therefore looked upon France as his home, was that the fares were paid through Buckingham Palace.'

Almost always, the Windsors travelled through Le Havre, arriving by limousine and an accompanying truck for the 'mountains' of luggage that went with them to or from their palatial Paris home. Less often, they travelled in a first-class compartment on the boat train.

The Duke always had unlimited access to the bridge, a prized and welcome gesture, and one never accorded to any other passenger. 'The Duke always came to the bridge in time for Bishop's Rock,' recalled Captain Robert Brooks, 'but rarely for New York or Le Havre. Evidently he liked to see England.'

Together, the Windsors only went ashore at Southampton once, in 1967, at the special invitation of the Duke's niece, Her Majesty Queen Elizabeth II, to attend a very special function in London, marking the centenary of the birth of Queen Mary, the Duke's mother, the Queen's grandmother and that very grand lady who died in 1953 and for whom the illustrious Cunard liner was named. While the well-known Windsor pugs went ashore earlier at Le Havre on this occasion, Commodore Alexanderson and Captain Brooks went to the ship's main reception foyer to greet Lord Louis Mountbatten, a member of the Royal Family and longtime friend of the Windsors. He was to officially greet his 'cousin', the former Edward VIII, and his American-born wife. A gleam-

Far left The Windsors, with Commodore Alexanderson, attending a party for some fellow passengers, a travelling party from Lake Erie Junior College. The date is 22 March 1964. (*Alexanderson Collection*)

Left The couple's first arrival at Southampton in many years: the Duke and Duchess preparing to disembark, on 5 June 1967, at the invitation of Her Majesty Queen Elizabeth II. The Windsors would travel up to London to attend the celebrations for the centenary of the birth of the late Queen Mary. (*Alexanderson Collection*)

The Queen had sent Lord Mountbatten to greet the Windsors officially at Southampton. He was welcomed aboard at the Ocean Terminal by Commodore Alexanderson. (*Alexanderson Collection*)

ing Rolls Royce delivered Mountbatten to the Ocean Terminal at Southampton and he was then officially welcomed aboard. Previously, he himself had once crossed on the American superliner. 'There were official greetings,' recalled the Commodore, 'and then we escorted him to the Duck Suite. After some brief chatter, we left them.'

United States Lines headquarters in New York stressed that the Windsors were always to receive the best care and be given the kindest and most respectful regard. 'We always addressed them as "His Highness" and "Her Highness",' according to the Commodore. 'Protocol is protocol.' In fact, the Duchess was never officially styled as 'Her Royal Highness'. This was denied her, and to the very end of her life, by the Royal Family. It remained a prime cause of the rift that existed between the Windsors of Paris and the Windsors of London. The Duke remained bitterly disappointed and, to the end of his life, was deeply saddened that his beloved wife could not be accorded official royal status. Official or not, however, he insisted that his wife be addressed as 'Her Royal Highness.' Failure to do so usually meant, at the very least, a frigid stare.

Chief Quartermaster Les Barton saw the Duke often, on the bridge of the *United States* during the dozens of crossings made by the legendary couple. 'I recall many afternoon chats with the Duke. We also met often in the U Deck pantry. He was lonely and especially liked to talk about ships. He always went personally to the pantry for hot water for his tea. But he never ever drank from anything else but "grandpa's teapot" [King Edward VII], which travelled with him.

'The Duchess spent all day in their three-room suite, and then received the hairdresser and manicurist in late afternoon. This was in preparation for the Commodore's cocktail party. The Windsors had had a special deal with the United States Lines. They would attend certain onboard parties and submit to photographers and later would always grant a press interview, which was held in the tourist class main lounge at the end of each voyage. They always had something to say and, of course, always looked the part. They were always superbly dressed and walked aboard or ashore with five pugs in tow. The dog collars had gold sovereigns in them, which were actually Edward VIII coins that were never released publicly. Once, I recall the Duchess called "David" and both a pug and the Duke came running! They occupied two separate suites with the dogs in the middle. He would walk across the centre sitting-room and always knocked on her door before entering.'

'The Windsors sometimes played bingo in the Main Lounge,' according to David Fitzgerald, the ship's chief purser. 'He liked to talk about ships mostly, the Royal Navy and other liners. She liked to talk about people, social things mostly. Sometimes, she liked to hear about fellow passengers, the little insights, and she was always fond of meeting "interesting" fellow passengers. I recall her special request to meet cosmetic queen Estée Lauder.

'The Windsors were always newsworthy and were very valuable passengers. They paid minimum fares for their first-class suites, which meant $340 compared to $1,200. The Duchess was always immaculate, always interesting and always seemed to intrigue the reporters. He was always very pleasant, but perhaps less extroverted with the press. I recall also that they always travelled with their own mahogany table, which had a round tilt top. They used this in their suite. Otherwise, their only other special request was to reserve 2-4 seats in the rear of the ship's theatre.'

'The Windsors were always courteous on the phone,' remembered Marjorie Marshall, senior telephone operator. 'The Duke was an absolute darling. I wrote a poem for their thirtieth wedding anniversary [1967] and was delighted to receive a personal thank you.

'Our telephone office was not far from the three suites on

U Deck that were occupied by these famed royal wanderers. Just opposite, they also took three inside cabins: one for his valet, one for her maid and one that served as an ironing room to press their clothes and personal linens. All United States Lines' linens, blankets and even draperies were replaced in their suites. Instead, the beds were done in very fine monogrammed linens, which were turned very deep over the blanket to expose their crest. Nearby, her exquisite bed jacket rested on a chair. The pugs were always there except at night when they slept in the top-deck kennels.

'When you walked into the Windsors' suite, you felt as if it had been lived in for fifteen or twenty years. Every table, every bureau was covered in silver and gold framed photos: his early years, the Duke in regimental dress, Queen Mary, wedding pictures and, of course, the Duchess herself. There was also an abundance of flowers of all kinds. It appeared to be a tropical garden. There were exotic animal skins draped across the sofas and little mementos everywhere: ashtrays, cigarette lighters, mounted crests. Really, you felt like an intruder. The dressing table was set out with jars and bottles, and also lined with sterling silver frames. All the combs and brushes were specially monogrammed. It was all very luxurious.'

The amount of luggage that accompanied the Windsors on board the United States was often talked about. 'Normally they crossed with about 30 pieces [other reports said as many as 95, even 98 pieces], mostly big, old fashioned Louis Vuitton wardrobe trunks,' remembered Ed Macy, the baggage master for the superliner. 'The big pieces were filled with clothes and household effects and once, during each crossing, their French secretary would do an on-board inventory. Especially, I remember their first trip with us, in 1952, when they sailed with 100 pieces of luggage and filled the entire species room.'

Of course, while they were unquestionably the most celebrated, the Windsors were not the only royal travellers that set sail in the United States. Commodore Alexanderson recalled a trip with Her Majesty Queen Frederika of Greece, in 1958. 'She boarded at Bremerhaven, after visiting her German relatives [the Queen was a Bavarian, who had married into the Greek Royal Family], but the US State Department was especially worried because of recent troubles in Greece. Security agents travelled with us and everything was very tight! All staff who came into contact with the Queen and her entourage were checked. The Queen was coming to the States to receive an honorary degree from Columbia University and also to witness the launching of a Niarchos tanker

Her Majesty Queen
Frederika of Greece
arriving at Pier 86,
New York, 1958.
(*United States Lines*)

at the Bethlehem Steel shipyards at Quincy, Massachusetts.
Her eldest daughter Sophia [now the Queen of Spain] was
to do the honours.

'His Serene Highness Prince Rainier of Monaco crossed
in 1955, to court film star Grace Kelly,' remembered Commodore Alexanderson. 'Later, he and Princess Grace crossed
with us while she was pregnant with Princess Caroline. I
invited the royal couple for a private visit to my quarters and
in turn they presented me with an official wedding picture,
which they kindly autographed for my daughter Linda.'

Perhaps the highest ranking political figures to sail in the
American supership were the two ex-presidents who had
held office during the *United States'* very earliest days of
development and construction. 'Harry Truman and his wife
Bess returned from Europe with us in 1956,' recalled the
Commodore, 'and were very nice. Inbound, in the Narrows

Former President and Mrs Dwight Eisenhower boarding the *United States* by tender. (*George Devol Collection*)

at 6.15 am, they came to the bridge to thank the senior officers for a good voyage.

'The Eisenhowers were also very cordial,' according to the Commodore. 'The ex-president, his wife Mamie, and his brother Milton were very undemanding, very easy passengers. They occupied a large suite, with two bedrooms and a sitting-room, and dined in the small private dining-room [with 43 seats and located on the Promenade Deck]. The Duke and Duchess of Windsor also used this room, but once during every crossing they would use the main dining-room and then always invited another couple to join them at a table for four. The Eisenhowers had sailed over in the *Queen Elizabeth* and then returned westbound on the *United States*. The president had visted her Majesty the Queen on British soil and then the battlefields of France before boarding the *United States* at Le Havre.'

Commodore Alexanderson had one less than happy recollection of a celebrity crossing:

Joseph P. Kennedy, the father of the president, was sailing with us. Oddly, Rose Kennedy was never with him. He used to sail alone with a couple of his buddies, one of his attorneys and so forth. They were all going over to France and they had a suite.

One evening, I received a call from our Chief Steward, Herman Mueller, who said, 'I'm sorry to bother you but we just had a call from Mr Kennedy and he wants me to fire his bedroom steward because his wristwatch is missing. It's the same watch that belonged to his son Joe, you know the one who was killed. Mr Kennedy is very much upset.'

I said, 'Okay, Herman, when he goes to dinner with his friends, get permission to go in there and you search the bedroom.' We had wall-to-wall carpeting and the watch could have easily bounced off the bed and slipped behind it.

Herman received permission and went in but there was no watch. It seems that Mr Kennedy had gone down to have a massage. The senior bedroom stewards in his group are all as honest as the day is long. That night, around 11 o'clock or so, I said to Herman, 'Okay, you haven't found the watch. Tomorrow morning, after Mr Kennedy gets up and goes to breakfast, before he leaves, you get permission from him and I want you to take the entire bed apart and get back in there.' These beds were secured. You couldn't see everything. Herman agreed. On the next morning, when he went to Mr Kennedy, who surprisingly said, 'Oh, that's all right. I found the watch. It was in the pocket of my robe.' He'd found it the night before but never said a word to us. They were all upset about the thing. He didn't have enough courtesy to call us. He didn't even apologize.

Other political figures included the then young Senator John F. Kennedy. Commodore Alexanderson recalled: 'He travelled with his wife Jacqueline, but because of his back problems, he used crutches throughout the trip.' Other political passengers who travelled aboard the United States Lines' flagship included Mrs Eleanor Roosevelt, General Matthew Ridgeway, Emperor Haile Selassie of Ethiopia, Prince Albert

Commodore Alexanderson after having just been specially honoured by President Tubman of Liberia, on board the *United States*, on 26 October 1961. (*Alexanderson Collection*)

of Belgium, and Chancellor Konrad Adenauer of West Germany. To this group, the Commodore added 'President Tubman of Liberia, whose bodyguard sat on the floor outside his suite. The president later presented Commodore Anderson, the Chief Engineer Bill Kaiser and myself with special decorations. We were made Commanders of the Order of Liberia and, during the ceremony, we were each given kisses on both cheeks.'

Others included Anthony Eden, the former British prime minister, who spent much of his voyage dictating letters to the ship's stenographer. Another, Madame Trujillo, widow of the deposed dictator of the Dominican Republic, was speaking at the United Nations on the morning of her sailing. Delayed in traffic while coming across town to Pier 86, the ship was held for thirty minutes, a rarity in United States Lines annals. The only other passenger for whom the *United States* was delayed was New York's Francis, Cardinal Spellman.

The great names of the film and stage worlds were often on board the *United States*. They were usually listed on the specially typed VIP first-class passenger lists, which were always included with special notations from the home office. These passengers were sometimes asked to meet reporters at the end of their crossing. There would be the customary string of prescribed questions (and at least one pointed refer-

The Commodore with Hollywood film actor Fred MacMurray in 1961. (*Alexanderson Collection*)

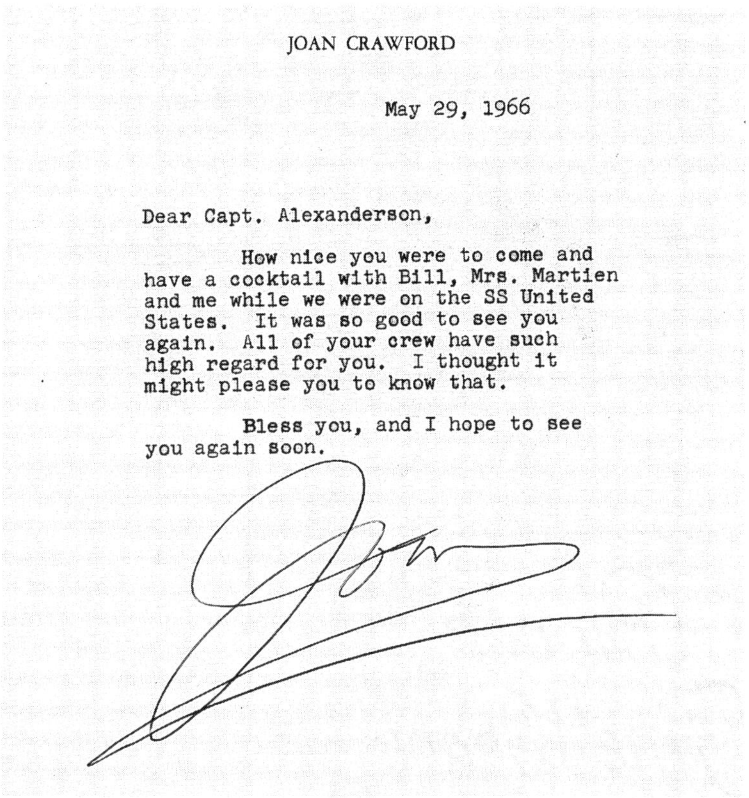

JOAN CRAWFORD

May 29, 1966

Dear Capt. Alexanderson,

How nice you were to come and have a cocktail with Bill, Mrs. Martien and me while we were on the SS United States. It was so good to see you again. All of your crew have such high regard for you. I thought it might please you to know that.

Bless you, and I hope to see you again soon.

A note from actress Joan Crawford. (*Alexanderson Collection*)

ence to the ship herself) and then a photo session, usually staged on one of the ship's outer decks. Screen goddess Rita Hayworth attracted particular press attention at the end of her crossing. She had been aboard less than a day out of Le Havre when, during her dinner, someone broke into her suite and stole her toilet seat. Of course, the cabin steward became the immediate suspect, but in the end he had a convincing alibi and the case was never resolved. Even at New York, the Customs inspectors were especially asked by United States Lines to check all passenger luggage. Another screen siren, Joan Crawford, came aboard often and always scrubbed her cabin bathroom herself. Ava Gardner brought along her own case of gin for the five-day trip.

Mary Pickford and her husband Buddy Rogers graciously shared their boat train compartment with a 'purser's aunt', whilst comic legend Harold Lloyd was especially thrilled when one of his old films was shown during the crossing. Actor James Stewart came to the purser's desk and bought his own boat train tickets; Bob Hope graciously entertained passengers in the first-class main lounge. Among many others, he offered a reverse joke: 'The *United States* is such

Actor John Wayne on the bridge of the *United States*, but this time with Commodore John Anderson. (*Alexanderson Collection*)

a marvellous ship, she could even be converted to a passenger ship in a few days!' When asked if he enjoyed the world's fastest ocean liner, comedian Jackie Gleason responded, 'Yes, I especially liked the food. I ate everything except the lifeboats!'

When comedienne Gracie Fields travelled on the *United States*, one of her sons was then working in the purser's department. Composer Irving Berlin declined an invitation for cocktails, but with gracious regrets, and singer Peggy Lee gave a voluntary performance in the main lounge. Circus mogul John Ringling North never left his suite in all of the five days, and the acrobatic Great Wallendas travelled in tourist class, insisting it was more comfortable.

Other passengers from the entertainment world who sailed aboard the *Big U* included: Greta Garbo, Kathrine Cornell, Cary Grant, John Wayne, Errol Flynn, Spencer Tracy, Katharine Hepburn, Marilyn Monroe, Merle Oberon, Rosalind Russell, Greer Garson, Kim Novak, Debbie Reynolds, Suzanne Pleshette, Victor Mature, Ray Milland, Charlton Heston, Alan Ladd, Sir Laurence Olivier, Rex Harrison, Red Skelton, Milton Berle, Jack Benny, Bud Abbott, Jack Lemmon, Jonathan Winters, George Jessel, Fernandel, Maurice Chevalier, Peter Finch, June Allyson, Ralph Bellamy, Yul Brynner, Marlon Brando, Sean Connery, John Carradine, David Janssen, Van Johnson, Cornel Wilde, Vera Ralston, Janet Leigh, Shirley MacLaine, Hermione Gingold, Robert Vaughn, Horst Bucholtz, Akim Tamiroff, Zero Mostel, Keir Dullea, Kevin McCarthy, Stanley Holloway, Lionel Jeffreys, Irene Pappas, Julie Wilson, Glenn Ford, Hope Lange, George Peppard, Elizabeth Ashley, Tony Martin, Cyd Charisse, Jane Wyman, Fred McMurray, Moss Hart, Kitty Carlisle, Steve Lawrence, Eydie Gorme, Vivian Vance, Walt Disney, Sam Goldwyn, David O. Selznick, Jennifer Jones, Ralph Edwards, William Boyd (Hopalong Cassidy), Tennessee Williams, Edward Albee, Sherwood Anderson, Al Capp, Leopold Stokowski, Eric Leinsdorf, Leonard Bernstein, Yehudi Menu-

A note from conductor Leopold Stokowski. (*Alexanderson Collection*)

hin, Irving Berlin, Mahalia Jackson, Elsa Maxwell, and the Vienna Boys' Choir.

Other notables included Salvador Dali travelling with his ocelot, which he sometimes kept in his cabin, and Henry Ford's daughters, Anne and Charlotte, both of whom kept asking for the Verandah Grill. Obviously, they had previously travelled on the Cunard *Queen*s. Oil billionaire John Paul Getty couldn't bear to tip, and both evangelist Billy Graham and gospel singer Mahalia Jackson asked that the bar be covered over during their religious presentations in the main lounge. Another famous guest was, in fact, a masterpiece. The *Mona Lisa* came on board in a specially air-conditioned container that was then placed in its own tightly guarded suite. She travelled westbound on the *France* and then homewards on the *United States*. During the crossing on the American liner, she even received invitations to a cocktail party. These were addressed to Mme Mona Lisa. Of course, she could not be removed and so the off-duty security guards attended in her place.

Because of her unique status as the world's fastest ocean liner and because of her American style, cuisine, and tone, the *United States* had considerable attraction for world celebrities, even to the very last days of her active career. Her only equals were the Cunard *Queen*s and the largest and grandest

Cocktails before dinner: another Hollywood icon, actor Jimmy Stewart, on Voyage No 328, westbound, September 1966. (*Alexanderson Collection*)

French liners of the day, namely the *Ile de France* and the *Liberté*, and later the *France*. Celebrities onboard the *Big U* were given the utmost care and consideration, perhaps the very finest at sea. This extended even to Customs, where they were specially expedited.

There were, of course, unexpected passengers on occasion. The Commodore recalled one incident:

A party in the ship's Navajo Room: singer Frances Langford is to the right of Commodore Alexanderson. The date is October 1960. (*Alexanderson Collection*)

During the summer, there were many college students travelling to Europe on the *United States*. Once, a day from Le Havre, a sailor told the Bos'n that a student had asked, 'How hard is it to get off the ship at Le Havre?' The sailor repeated the story to the Chief Purser, then he, the Bos'n, the Master-at-Arms, and the Chief Officer went to find that student. There were two of them onboard as stowaways, and both were questioned by the Executive Officer and put into the brig. We reported this to the New York office, and the boys' parents were contacted in Minnesota. On our westbound trip, a call came from one of the boys from his mother. The Radio Officer listened in. She said, 'They can't put you in jail. I'm going to see Senator Mondale. I won't pay your fare since they have you in the brig.' Before we arrived at New York, she called him again. 'Do you know what you've done?' she said. 'We have paid your fare but you are in serious trouble.' When we arrived at New York, the FBI gave them a real going over and told them to stay out of trouble. Later, it turned out that they had the fare for their trip after all.

Keeping the
Big U Fit

'It was just like a grease job on your car!' according to Gene
Yaeger, the former manager of commercial ship repair at the
Newport News Shipbuilding & Dry Dock Co yards in Virginia. He was describing the annual overhaul given to the
commercial pride of that facility, the *United States*. 'She would
come down in December, normally including the Christmas
holiday, and then be ready in time for an early January crossing. [In later years, this was changed to November, over the
Thanksgiving holiday, as the ship would have to sail from
New York on a Christmas-New Year's cruise.] She would be
cleaned and painted, her bottom scraped and the sea chests
cleaned [sea chests are the openings where water for the
machinery comes in and out.] Also, there would always be
fractures in the shaft tunnel that would need to be repaired.
Actually, we knew where all the fractures would be from
year to year—they would repeat. It was the same with the
America [which also went to Newport News and sometimes
at the same time as the *United States*]. We would know all
the rivets that had to be replaced from year to year.'

Gene Yaeger added, 'We worked round the clock on the
Big U. We had to change propellers. Also, the bow had to
be built-up, 2 ft thick, because during the course of the year,
it would be eaten away. We used epoxy. This changed the
configuration of the bow. Similarly, on the *America*, there
was always cracking just forward of the house on the starboard side.'

There was always a set procedure for the annual overhaul
of the *United States*. Commodore Alexanderson added, 'Captain "Kiddo" Edwards [the senior Virginia pilot] used to fly
to New York and then sail with us to the shipyard. It was
an overnight trip and we would have about half of the crew
still aboard. There would be a minimum delay coming into
the Hampton Roads area and then he [Captain Edwards]

would take over at Cape Henry and pilot the ship to the final approaches to the shipyard. The yard tug *Huntington* joined us off the coal piers. Captain Ambrose of the tug would come aboard then and take her in. Other tugs assisted, of course, as we berthed in the graving dock.'

A detailed account of the docking of the *United States* was published in *Shipyard Bulletin*, the journal of the Newport News Shipbuilding & Dry Dock Co, in their November 1967 issue:

'It's a fine day for puttin' her in dock,' said shipyard tugmaster M. L. Ambrose as we boarded the tug *Huntington* at 9.30 am at Shipway 10.

No one could have argued with the veteran captain and pilot for the day was clear with only a slight breeze, and a calm James River. And, in contrast with some past years, there would be plenty of manoeuvring room on the port side of the liner since no aircraft carrier flight deck was protruding into Shipway 10 from the adjacent dock.

Twenty minutes after we boarded the *Huntington*, shipway 10 was ready to host its famous guest: the 187 keel blocks on which the hull of the ship would rest had been carefully set into place on the floor of the slipway, the 960 ft long dock had been filled, the gate moored securely at the outboard end of Shipway 11 and eleven 60 ft long timber fenders had been secured along the Shipway's walls as a precaution. The latter two operations involved the *Huntington* and were in progress as we boarded.

Our first radio contact with the *United States* came at 9.50am as Captain Ambrose steered the *Huntington* south along the shipyard waterfront. A radioman on the giant liner reported that his ship was approaching Old Point Comfort. Ambrose responded, 'You can ease her along since we have the tugs reserved for 11 am.' This plan was acceptable to the *United States*.

The *Huntington* moved forward toward Pier 4 where we took aboard two Riggers Department supervisors who would assist in the docking operations.

By 10.05 am we were heading out into the James for our rendezvous with the *United States*. After pausing briefly while Captain Ambrose gave positioning instructions to the captain of the tug *Michael J. McAllister*, we moved south along the Newport News waterfront. By 10.20 am, we were idling off the general cargo piers.

Captain Ambrose, who would 'pilot' the *United States* into the dock, chose these minutes to reflect on his 'kinship' with the superliner. It dates from the ship's delivery in 1952.

'I think I've helped put her in dock every time she's been back since we delivered her,' he declared.

A quick count revealed that this would be the fifteenth time that he had docked the colossus.

Turning next to the importance of high tide in the docking procedure, Ambrose said, 'Of course our schedules are set up to take

advantage of the current so that we have the highest water in the dock. We like to work about an hour ahead of slack tide,' he said.

At 10.25 am, the unmistakable red, white and blue stacks of the *United States* became visible to us for the first time as the liner steamed through Hampton Roads. Five minutes later, her full 990 ft length came into view as she swung past the Newport News boat harbour and the Chesapeake & Ohio coal piers. Two other tugboats, which would assist in the docking, would flank her as they moved up the river. From Ambrose, they received radio telephone instructions for their assignments in the task ahead.

As the *United States* loomed larger, Captain Ambrose radioed her that we might soon be 'crossing her bow' to take some pictures.

'I thought you might see us and get a little disturbed,' he quipped.

Chuckling, the liner's radioman responded, 'The Commodore says to tell you that we don't get disturbed! Thank you for calling.'

And 'OK, buddy' from Ambrose closed the exchange.

By 10:40 am, the *United States* was 300 yards dead ahead of the *Huntington*. A request from the tug brought forth a trio of deafening greetings from the liner's deep-throated whistle.

Rendezvous was next on the schedule. Ambrose steered up hard against the starboard side of the *United States*. A short ladder was raised to an opening on B Deck. Several of the liner's crewmen were waiting to greet us and tossed the first heaving lines to a waiting shipyard crew. These were pulled back aboard and secured to the ship. Eight of these lines, four on a side, were manned by gangs of Riggers who help control the drift of the ship as it moves into the dock.

The bow of the *United States* pushed across the sill and into the dock at 11:25 am. From this point on, Dockmaster W.C. Thomas and his crew would team with Ambrose to assure a successful docking.

During the next 20 minutes, the most crucial of the operation, Captain Ambrose was a picture of confidence.

His intense facial expressions reflected the magnitude of this job. He peered over the wing—to check our progress—looking down, then forward, then aft. His loud and clear instructions for engine operation are relayed by telegraph from wheelhouse to engine room. They included such commands as 'All engines slow astern'. 'Slow ahead on all engines'. 'Slow astern on port engine'. 'Dead slow ahead'. All commands are related to the delicate manoeuvring of this 53,000-ton vessel precisely and accurately into the dock.

At 11:28 am, Captain Ambrose instructs one tugmaster to shift his vessel from the port quarter to the starboard to help correct a slight drifting of the liner's bow. All engines on the liner were temporarily stopped at 11:28 am. Four minutes later, Ambrose barked out a command: 'Dead slow ahead on starboard', as they started up again.

Slowly, but surely, the *United States* at 11:35 am was nearing the half-way mark in its docking. The tug *Huntington* stood at the out-

Opposite It's 10:40 am and Tugmaster Ambrose begins manoeuvring the tug *Huntington* toward the approaching *United States*. (*Newport News Shipbuilding & Dry Dock Co*)

SS United States

Right 10:48 am: tugmaster becomes pilot as he boards the mighty *United States*. (*Newport News Shipbuilding & Dry Dock Co*)

Far right The *Big U* approaches the graving dock. (*Newport News Shipbuilding & Dry Dock Co*)

Far right It is now 11:40 am; the *United States* is moving into the graving dock, which has been flooded, while the tug *Huntington* holds the 990-ft long liner away from the dock itself. (*Newport News Shipbuilding & Dry Dock Co*)

SS United States

board end of the shipway hard against the hull of the ship. At 11:37 am, responding to a question about the progress of the docking, Ambrose replied 'Everything just lovely.'

Two minutes later, he again commanded that all engines be stopped. The forward movement of the ship was now hardly noticeable until you looked overboard. We were still moving. At 11.41 am, Captain Ambrose directed that the engines be at slow ahead as the ship moved well into the dock.

By 11:48 am, the giant liner was as far forward in the dock as she needed to go. Her 990 ft length overhung both ends of the shipway. At dock's edge, Dockmaster Thomas and his crew are taking sightings at the bow of the ship and at frame number 200. This important task is done to assure proper alignment of the vessel when it settles onto the keel blocks as the shipway is pumped dry.

By 11:50 am, the *United States* is docked.

As he leaves the bridge, Commodore Alexanderson thanks Ambrose for a 'nice job' and bids him farewell.

Asked how it went as we were leaving the liner, Ambrose smiled and said, 'Good weather, good tugs and a good crew.'

The busy Pilot, now turned Tugmaster, was not yet completely finished with his *United States* assignment. During the next 45 minutes, at the helm of the *Huntington*, he would direct the return of the Shipway 10 gate to its location and aid in the removal of

Opposite The long bow section as she makes the approach. (*Newport News Shipbuilding & Dry Dock Co*)

Pilot Ambrose, with Commodore Alexanderson to his right, is about to radio-telephone some orders to the five assisting tugs. (*Newport News Shipbuilding & Dry Dock Co*)

An impressive aerial view as nearly three-quarters of the liner is already within the graving dock. (*Newport News Shipbuilding & Dry Dock Co*)

the protective fenders.

Pumping water from the dock began as soon as the gate was in place and by 2 pm, water had been pumped to the 23 ft draft mark on the ship. It remained at this level for the next eight and one-half hours while the liner's turbines cooled. Pumping resumed at 10:30 pm and by the next morning, the *United States* was high and dry and ready for work on her hull.

The drydocking of a ship, whether it is the *United States* or another of the 130 ships calling at the Shipyard each year, is an eloquent exercise in teamwork on the part of man, machine and nature. On November 3, with the successful docking of the nation's premier passenger ship, that team chalked up another first class performance.

Not all dockings at the shipyard were quite the same, however. 'At least once,' recalled Commodore Alexanderson, 'the nuclear carrier *Enterprise* was in the next dock, but with an enormous overhang by her flight deck. Consequently, all the port lifeboats on the *United States* had to be removed before going into the graving dock. It was fine-tune docking. There was very little space between the carrier and the *United States*. Luckily, Captain Ambrose was one of the finest ship handlers I have ever encountered.'

The *United States* seemed to dominate the shipyard for those three or four weeks of overhaul. Those towering red,

Opposite The shipyard's dockmaster signals with a post to check accurate alignment of the liner. (*Newport News Shipbuilding & Dry Dock Co*)

Below 16 January 1963: the *United States* and the *America* together for their winter overhauls. (*Michael Shernoff Collection*)

Right The 53,000-ton *United States* and the 87,000-ton nuclear carrier *Enterprise* in the graving docks. (*Newport News Shipbuilding & Dry Dock Co*)

Far right Maintenance on the tallest funnels of their day. (*Frank O. Braynard Collection*)

Below far right Tight squeeze: a US Navy carrier on the left; the *United States* on the right. (*United States Lines*)

white, and blue funnels stood out, especially at night when they continued to be floodlit. Cranes hovered about, scaffolding and ladders were in place, and painting crews with brushes on long poles were busy at work on the outer skin of the great ship. Some shipyard crews had been involved in the original construction and like almost everyone else, took great pride and real satisfaction in her. She was, after all, the pride of the American merchant marine, the fastest liner of all time, one of the largest (between 1952 and 1969, only four other liners, the *Queen Mary, Queen Elizabeth, France,* and finally the *Queen Elizabeth 2,* exceeded her in size), and, of course, she was something of a maritime wonder-ship, a sea-going technological marvel. Some, perhaps slightly more enthusiastic, liked to think of her as flawless. Many, many other ships came to Newport News for repairs and overhaul, but none, perhaps not even those staggering Navy carriers with the breadth of their flight decks and their four- and five-thousand crewmembers, seemed to create quite the same excitement in those years. Beyond the main gates of the shipyard, there was also always interest and enthusiasm, when the *United States* was in port. There was customarily a newspaper notice announcing her arrival and

then, of course, there was chatter amongst the workers, their families, and friends. One can just visualize a shipyard painter, returning home after a day shift and telling his children about the mighty hull of the world's fastest ocean liner. One can just see their brightened eyes! Again, it was part of the special interest, the sense of pride in that superlative ship which was Newport News-built. She was assuredly the very finest passenger ship the shipyard had ever produced, their most newsworthy creation, perhaps their very best commercial project.

There was at least one other practice that took place during these drydocking periods. According to Commodore Alexanderson, 'The ship's crew used to buy inexpensive booze in Europe and then sell it to shipyard workers at $2 a bottle. Once, someone sent an anonymous letter to the local Customs and an investigation developed. The booze was stored in an empty tourist-class cabin. Suddenly, the crew tried to get rid of the evidence. They dumped it as fast as they could do in the James River. Always, there were all kinds of "rackets" going on—like gambling and loansharking. But yet if an officer tried to investigate, word passed down—and like lightning!—and the game or whatever broke up by the time the Executive Officer reached the lower decks.'

Opposite The four propellers of the world's fastest liner. (*Frank O. Braynard Collection*)

Work continues around the clock: a night view of the *United States* at her shipyard 'wet berth'. (*Alexanderson Collection*)

'The annual overhaul included the annual Coast Guard inspection—a check of the boats and life preservers,' added Commodore Alexanderson. 'We lowered all the boats and placed them in the water. There was work around the clock, and never any sense of noticeable silence. She always went to Newport News, but in the very beginning, she drydocked twice a year and on three occasions, to save time, she went to the graving dock at Bayonne, New Jersey, then operated by the US Navy and located on a western peninsula off New York's Lower Bay.

'We kept a spare set of propellers at Newport News. Initially, these were bronze propellers, but these began to crack on the edges. Later, we changed to nylite props, which were heavier and stronger. The bronze had better performance, but the nylite proved more durable.'

'There was always very tight shipyard security, at least prior to 1968 [William Francis Gibbs died in September 1967],' remembered Commodore Alexanderson. 'Mr Gibbs had sent letters to Newport News Shipyard with exact instructions and details. There were to be absolutely no photographs! No one but no one went to the engine room—with the obvious exception of the engine room staff and chief officers. I do believe, however, that this mania for secrecy was more Gibbs than either the Pentagon or the shipyard.'

Once the repairs, the changes, the painting, and the inevitable house-cleaning were complete, the *United States* would be, much like Humpty Dumpty, put back together again and readied for her return to service. She would again be in perfect order—every sofa and chair and cocktail table in place, every bed neatly made, every pile of restaurant china in order. 'Outward to New York, Captain Edwards again took her to Cape Henry,' recalled the Commodore. 'At this time, we would adjust the compasses. This was done by one of the Smolas, local compass adjusters, assisted by ship's officers. He would travel with us up to New York.'

With several days to spare, for provisioning, loading and refuelling, the *United States* would wait, at the north side of Pier 86, in preparation for her next voyage. Then, with her full staff returned to duty and with passengers again filling her lounges, corridors, and cabins, she would return to her intended role: voyaging in the open sea. But, as the ship sailed into the later 1960s, in that changing era of Moon landings, a military struggle in South-east Asia, and inner city turmoil, time was running short for the world's fastest ocean liner.

Chapter 7

Finished With Engines

October 1958 was the great turning-point in transatlantic travel. Like many other writers, I have written before of this pivotal date. It was then that the first jet flew the North Atlantic and the fate of the ocean liner, particularly on that run, was sealed. Quite simply, the jets were there to stay. It all became a matter of hours rather than days—and consequently, and within six months no less, the airlines secured (perhaps snatched is a better word) 63 per cent of all traffic: 1,539,934 went by air, 881,894 by sea. In fact, even earlier, in 1957, aircraft had, for the first time, carried more passengers than the Atlantic liners. Corporate directors and board room agendas took little serious notice at first, however. The comment that came from the Cunard Line's marble-clad Liverpool headquarters just about summed-up everyone else's reaction: 'Flying is just a fad. There will always be enough passengers that prefer to go by sea.' A fad, indeed!

But if the Atlantic liner trade would decline steadily, in fact grow more and more desolate, especially at the onset of the swinging sixties, the figures for 1957-8—and in all fairness to those boardroom pundits—were still encouraging. Both the *United States* and the *America*, while working on their regular, but quite separate patterns, were continuing to carry impressive loads of passengers. The *United States* was still a blazing success, still the most popular single liner on the Atlantic run. The *America*, smaller, slower, and approaching her twentieth year, and therefore steaming into middle age for ocean liners (especially American-flag ones), still had a very loyal following.

In the late 1950s, despite the airline invasion, the building of new transatlantic liners was still a very real possibility. There had even been talk about a comparable and equally powerful 'sistership' or 'running mate' to the *United States*.

There was the military value to consider of such a ship's potential as a trooper; and then, of course, at least for a few more years, there was the possibility that she might earn her way as a commercial passenger liner, and also as a profit-making winter cruiseship.

Bids were actually requested by the United States Lines and then sent by three well-known American shipbuilders: Newport News, of course, and also the New York Shipbuilding Corporation at Camden, New Jersey (which had built the United States Lines' sisters *Washington* and *Manhattan* in the early 1930s and the Bethlehem Steel Company and Quincy, Massachusetts (builders of the sisters *Independence* and *Constitution* in 1950-1). The bids for a new supership ranged from $109 to $117 million. In brief comparison, the French were planning their very large *France*, at 66,000 tons, and she would cost $80 million. Of course, she would not have quite the same enormous speed capability or extensive military components, but American shipbuilding costs were always considerably higher than anywhere else, and so were operational costs. Quite simply, it was more difficult financially for a US-flag firm to operate a passenger ship than a foreign-flag competitor.

The United States Lines were very interested in a new superliner to replace the ageing *America* and perhaps even as the long overdue competitor for Cunard's two-ship weekly express runs with the *Queens*. Some saw the *Mary* and the *Elizabeth* as ageing greyhounds, and, when their time came, perhaps two American superliners could fill their role. But, realistically, the United States Lines was in no way able to afford such a new speed queen. They needed US government help—and considerable help at that. A severe blow came, in spring 1957, when some $95 million was eliminated by Congress in President Eisenhower's proposed maritime budget. This would have been the money, at least part of it, for a 'second' *United States*. Not all was lost, however, and the question of a second superliner was not put to rest completely. Even if the airlines carried more passengers—and in 1957, for the first time, they carried more than all liners combined—the *United States* was still averaging a most impressive 3,000 travellers per roundtrip.

In 1958, there was more talk of a new superliner, including some very specific improvements to such a vessel by William Francis Gibbs. But projected costs, still steadily increasing, were making the possibilities look less and less likely. Another blow came from the SIU, the Seafarers International Union, and rival to the NMU, the National Maritime Union, which serviced the *United States*. The SIU

Opposite A final gathering: Christmas cruise departures from New York, in December 1968: (from top to bottom) *Queen Anna Maria*, *Empress of Canada* (just arriving), Cunard freighter *Ivernia*, *Leonardo da Vinci*, *France*, *United States*, *Victoria*, *Oceanic*, and *Homeric*. (*Flying Camera Inc*)

insisted that spending over $100 million on a new super-liner was impractical. They said that such monies would be better spent on small cargo ships, for companies with which the SIU had manning contracts.

The *United States* logged her millionth mile, inbound off the Statue of Liberty, on 30 September 1958. It was a special moment in the ship's history; but two days later her eastbound crossing, with 1100 passengers, had to be cancelled because of a labour dispute with the Masters, Mates and Pilots, another powerful union. These strikes, which would continue into the 1960s with almost timed regularity, would be among the most decisive blows to the demise of the world's fastest passenger ship. How disappointing for a passenger expecting to sail in the pride of the American merchant fleet to find themselves transferred to the likes of the *Queen Elizabeth*, the *Liberté*, or the *Statendam*—or, more disheartening still, to a Pan Am or TWA flight, departing not from 'Luxury Liner Row' with champagne, streamers, and the magic of sailing past the Manhattan skyline, but instead from a darkened tarmac, thirty-odd miles from the city, at Idlewild Airport (renamed John F. Kennedy International in late 1963).

Even after this disruptive strike was settled, optimism from the 1 Broadway offices was diminished. The mood was changing, though gradually. Talk and speculation about a new superliner dwindled further, especially as the company made it clear that the *America*, soon to be twenty years old, was in very fine condition and could easily continue in service for many years to come. Realistically, the issue of the new ship was dead, and even the *America* was running short on time. In less than five years, by 1964, she would be retired and sold off to the Greeks.

Again, in 1960, and just for the record, there was absolutely no provision in government funds for a superliner. But, simultaneously, there were schemes for a *United States*-type liner for the transpacific run as well. She would sail out of San Francisco and Los Angeles to Hawaii, Japan, Hong Kong, and the Philippines for the American President Lines as the 43,000-ton, 956-ft long *President Washington*. She would, it was proposed, carry 1,450 passengers in three classes. There were even whispers that the American Export Lines wanted a third ship for their Mediterranean services. But these, like the companion to the *United States*, would never materialize. They would be too expensive and, as some US government officials argued, less and less useful as wartime troopers. 'New liners as troopships,' protested at least one Congressman, 'would be nothing more than "sitting ducks" to Soviet bombers!'

1960 was a decisive year for the future of the *United States*. She began carrying fewer and fewer passengers. In fact, for an early January crossing, the United States Lines, which had customarily released figures, made no mention of the actual numbers. Indeed, they were too embarrassing. The airlines were taking more and more passengers and even the dependants of the American military forces, who were intended from the very start to fill a considerable number of the ship's cabins, were defecting to speedier aircraft. The overall picture was growing dim. There was even the very first discussions of possibly converting the *United States* to a cruiseship, or at least making more provision in her for winter trips to the Caribbean and elsewhere. Up until this time, she had never cruised.

On 1 September 1960, the United States Dept of Commerce announced, in yet another blow to the United States Lines, that the contract to carry military dependants to and from Europe in the *United States* and *America* was terminated. Suddenly, every cabin had to be sold commercially. Never before had the company been faced with such a task. A large advertising, sales and promotional campaign was mounted: 'The route of the unrushables', the glories of crossing in the speed queen *United States*, was one theme. The comfort, the food, the care, even the benefits of the sea air, were brought to travellers' attention like never before, at least not since the lean years of the Depression in the early 1930s. These were desperate times for the Atlantic liners, their last great battle.

Additionally, it was decided to convert the *America* from her three-class (first, cabin, and tourist) configuration to a two-class (first and tourist) ship. Her tourist quarters increased consequently from 165 to 530 berths. Tourist space was certainly far more saleable at the time. More serious plans were drawn up to adapt the *United States* for winter cruising. Ideas included creating a permanent outdoor pool in place of the aft cabin-class lounge on Upper Deck. The tourist-class dining room would be removed and all tourist cabins would be enlarged and given that prized amenity—especially to demanding American cruise passengers—private toilets and showers. Conservative estimates were put at $15 million to alter the *United States*. Little else happened, however. This refit, like a possible running-mate and that American President superliner, slipped into a sort of permanent limbo. There was a growing feeling that big, class-divided trans-ocean liners were like 'dinosaurs'. Their days were numbered. Barely a soul wanted to stake his reputation in supporting further expenditures, especially at the

171

United States Lines and especially without government funds.

More problems and further changes continued. The United States Lines, in a cost-saving effort to reduce port fees, had the *United States* officially remeasured in 1961, from 53,329 to 51,988 gross tons. Soon after, in another noteworthy decision, a February sailing to Europe in the *America* had to be cancelled to save money. A scant 350 passengers had been booked on that trip. They were offered space on other sailings instead. A new brochure cover showed the *United States* steaming beneath a Pan Am jet clipper. Air-sea tours, one way by ship and the other by air, were the future—at least for the immediate future.

The United States Lines wanted, almost desperately, to send both the *United States* and *America* on more lucrative off-season cruises. US government subsidy regulations insisted, however, that these ships could not deviate from their intended service, no matter how unprofitable. The United States Lines management protested more and more and finally, in November 1961, the *America* was permitted to make her first cruise in well over a decade, a five-day voyage to Bermuda over the Thanksgiving holiday. I recall sailing that same weekend aboard Germany's *Hanseatic* and thinking how odd it was that the *America* was cruising!

Earlier, in that June, both the *United States* and *America* were hit by another strike. Laid-up, it was the first time since her construction, nearly a decade earlier, that the *United States* was 'shut down' completely. Voyages were again cancelled, passengers were reassigned (to other steamship lines, mostly foreign-flag, and to the airlines), with the overall effect that the once sterling image of the United States Lines and its passenger liners was tarnished, perhaps permanently. Passengers as well as the all-important travel agents had less and less faith in booking both the *United States* and *America*. Patriotic feelings were not quite enough.

Finally, with government permission in hand, the *United States* was allowed to make her first cruises, in January-February 1962. Both would be two-week trips out of New York, calling at Nassau, St Thomas, Trinidad, Curacao, and Cristobal. She would be one of the largest liners ever scheduled for such cruises and, of course, these were to be her 'maiden voyage' of sorts to the tropics. A portable pool was fitted on the aft deck, the tourist-class quarters were closed off, and minimum fares were posted at $520.

This new year also witnessed another sensible decision: teaming the operation of the *United States* with the new *France*. Like the Cunard *Queens*, they would sail on alternate weeks. Realistically, however, the *France*, being newer and with the celebrated French Line reputation for service, luxury, and their flawless kitchens, had the competitive edge. The *United States* continued to carry fewer and fewer passengers.

There were still more strikes, including one that sent both the *United States* and *America* to lay-up at the Newport News yards. United States Lines also publicly revealed for the first time that it cost a staggering $20 million a year to run the *United States*: $7 million for crew (the bootblack, for example earned an impressive $302 monthly); $3.5 million for fuel; $3.3 million for stores, supplies and subsistence; $1 million for brokerage commissions; $1 million for union contributions; and $2.4 million for port expenses. No other liner cost as much. Consequently, every possible cost-cutting method was considered. Again, the tonnage was remeasured (dropping to 44,893 during 1963) to save port fees.

United States Lines again proposed that improvements be made to the *United States*, especially in view of her more frequent winter cruises and, more specifically, to compete more successfully with the *France*. They proposed that private showers and toilets in tourist-class cabins be installed on the American flagship (most of those on the French liner had such amenities). Projected cost of these alterations was placed at $1.2 million. Regrettably, however, the US government again denied the request. Washington still had the final say on almost all aspects of the *United States*.

But the worst blow yet, perhaps the great turning point, came on 14 September 1963. Hours before she was to make her regular noontime departure from New York's Pier 86, a labour dispute erupted aboard the *America*. Unsettled, management decided to cancel the sailing. Her anxious and worried passengers were sent ashore and, once again, the United States Lines passenger department had to make alternate arrangements for them—some to other ships, others to the airlines. Management was furious and, so it would seem, this dispute sparked a severe reaction. The *America* was laid up for six months, with all sailings, transatlantic crossings, and winter cruises cancelled. The curtain was beginning, if ever so slowly, to close—not only for the 23-year-old ship but for the 11-year-old *United States* as well. The strike was started by an onboard jurisdictional dispute over the use of a toilet. It all was clouded with racial and ethnic overtones. Indeed, it was a very nasty and embarrassing affair.

The *America* was laid up for a time, then returned for a rather abbreviated final season on the North Atlantic before being sold off to the Greeks, in November 1964, to become an Australian migrant ship. Thereafter, the *United States* worked alone, adequately handling the continually dwindling numbers of passengers that would come her way. She continued to offer her transatlantic crossings, interspersed with winter season cruises; but she was becoming increasingly expensive to operate and was facing yet more strikes, labour difficulties, and disruptions. In the summer of 1965, the *United States* experienced her worst strike yet, from 1 July until 26 August, and so missed the peak of the summer Atlantic season. Quietly, she sat through those warm-weather weeks at Pier 86. Over 9,000 passengers were stranded and $3 million in revenues lost. Her image and, more especially, her future were further compromised. On the next sailing, in late August, she set off with a rather dismal 800 or so passengers—all of them being looked after by over a thousand costly crewmembers.

Times had indeed grown worse for the Atlantic liner fleet. American Export, for example, had the *Independence* and *Constitution* restyled mostly for cruising, but then they lost interest and abandoned the passenger business entirely. The Dutch were down to one liner, the *Nieuw Amsterdam*, until she too was retired from Atlantic crossings in 1971. And lastly, Cunard had retired all of its fleet including the veteran *Queen Mary* and *Queen Elizabeth*. Within that British fleet, seven liners were replaced by one: the brand new *Queen Elizabeth 2*, which was commissioned in the spring of 1969. Together with the *France* and the *United States*, these ships would create the final trio of superliners on the North Atlan-

Fading light on an autumn afternoon: the *United States* on her final call at New York, just hours before her last departure from her home port. (*Fred Rodriguez*)

Final arrival at
Newport News.
(*Alexanderson Collection*)

tic. But time was running short for both of the last-named ships.

During 1966, even though the *United States* made her fastest eastbound crossing (33.06 knots) since her maiden year and even though she statistically carried more passengers than any other Atlantic liner, including the *France*, her future prospects continued to grow dim. Her transatlantic schedule, the pace of her turnarounds in port, were accelerated to maximise profits and also to create a wider range of dates for her prospective passengers. Her cruises became more imaginative. Her longest winter trip yet set sail in February 1968, a month-long run to Curacao, Rio de Janeiro, Dakar,

At her birthplace for what was at first thought to be a customary overhaul. (*Alexanderson Collection*)

Teneriffe, Gibraltar, and Lisbon.

During 1968, the US government—embroiled in the political difficulties in South-east Asia—asked Americans to curtail travel to Europe in an effort to save dollars. This was yet another blow, to the struggling United States Lines sales and marketing staff. At the same time, the company was sold to Walter Kidde & Co, a conglomerate, and shortly after consummation of the deal, rumours began in earnest that the *United States* was nearing her end. Quite simply, the new Kidde regime at New York did not want her. The age of big Atlantic liners was finished, at least as far as they were concerned. She was too expensive, so they thought, and facing a very uncertain future, not only in the rapidly dwindling Atlantic trade but also in the increasingly competitive cruise industry as well. There was that persistent problem of high costs for American liners, particularly with crew wages.

Commodore Alexanderson saw the ship through these last troubled times. 'The big planes were a terrific blow, certainly a lot cheaper, to our operation. The decision to retire the *United States* was obviously not as abrupt as we might think. It was long in the planning stage, perhaps even before the long cruise to Capetown (January 1969). The saviours of the ship, William Francis Gibbs (who died in 1967) and General Franklin (who had retired), were gone. The Walter Kidde owners had all new management.

'Labour had a big part as well,' recalled the Commodore, 'They wanted pay raises and more and more demands. These were demands made not on me, but on United States Lines management. Management always backed down and gave in. It is amazing to look back at all those men who, in the end, lost their jobs, many of whom were there from Voyage No 1. They were loyal. They loved the ship.'

'Rumours of retirement began in full force in the summer of 1969,' according to Quartermaster Les Barton. 'But most of us felt it would not really happen. Those later years were also filled with scandal and corruption. Materials, for example, sent to the *United States* actually went to other United States Lines ships, but were charged to the liner's accounts. In the end, management claimed that the *Big U* lost as much as $11 million annually. The management were only interested in making money, not in prestige or propaganda.

Her refit cancelled, the ship silent and lonely — the *Big U* at her shipyard berth, in December 1969. (*United States Lines*)

Brochure covers for two cruises that never took place: the Autumn Seaventure, scheduled for November 9th 1969, which would have gone across the mid-Atlantic for 21 days; and the ship's longest yet and her first visit into the Pacific, 55 days to the South Seas, Australia and then the Far East, which was set for the following January 21st and would last 55 days. (*Michael Shernoff Collection*)

They really weren't interested, even if the government might increase the subsidy. It was no use! The gossip mounted by early November.'

'The writing was on the wall months ahead,' added Chief Purser David Fitzgerald. 'Many of us felt the ship would never come out of drydock (in November), even if we were planning the big Pacific cruise (scheduled for January 1970). Of course, escalating costs and strikes were the biggest reasons and also testy Union regulations, especially overtime and shifting. There was also the problem of extra expenses being added to the *Big U*. Then, of course, the future for passengers wasn't bright and there was less expertise in the "new" management.'

In September 1969, a headline in the *New York Times* read: LINER UNITED STATES IS BEAUTIFUL, FAST, POWERFUL AND BROKE. Captain Robert Brooks felt that 'first and foremost, the reason for the demise of the *United States* was the decline of US government operating subsidies. And, of course, union demands were increasing as United States Lines was simultaneously decreasing. The unions were so difficult, so unhelpful. The ship received an annual US government subsidy of $12 million, but, by 1969, was losing $4.8 million. The losses would increase. A new, extended government subsidy was not granted when it came up for renewal in late 1969. The evidence was against her. The *United States* was subsidized by the Federal Government, in 1969, at the rate of $400 for every passenger ticket sold. This couldn't last.'

Abruptly, in flash orders from the New York office, a 9 November cruise (a 21-day trip to Bermuda, Lisbon, Madeira, Teneriffe, Dakar, St Thomas, and Nassau) was cancelled and the ship was to go instead to Newport News, supposedly for an early overhaul. Consequently, the 25 October sailing from New York to Bremerhaven via Le Havre and Southampton would prove her last trip. It was Voyage No 400. Reservations were, however, still being accepted at the time for the 16-day Christmas Caribbean cruise and for that grand 55-day Pacific cruise (her longest cruise ever and her first voyage in the Pacific Ocean, sailing from New York to the Panama Canal, Pitcairn Island, Auckland, Wellington, Sydney, Hong Kong, Kobe, Yokohama, Honolulu, San Francisco, Acapulco, and return to New York via the Canal).

Souvenir log card of the final voyage.

QUADRUPLE SCREW TURBINE STEAMSHIP
"UNITED STATES"
COMMODORE L. J. ALEXANDERSON
Rear Admiral, U.S.N.R.

Abstract of Log **Voyage 400, Westbound**

From BREMERHAVEN to NEW YORK, via SOUTHAMPTON and LE HAVRE

Left Weser L.V., 2:57 p.m., C.E.T., Nov. 1, 1969   Arrived Nab Tower, 6:45 a.m., B.S.T., Nov. 2, 1969
Distance, WESER L.V. to NAB TOWER: 467 Miles
Steaming Time: 15 Hours, 48 Minutes — Average Speed: 29.56 Knots

Left Nab Tower, 2:42 p.m., B.S.T., Nov. 2, 1969   Arrived Havre L.V., 5:18 p.m., C.E.T., Nov. 2, 1969
Distance, NAB TOWER to LE HAVRE L.V.: 75 Miles
Steaming Time: 2 Hours, 36 Minutes — Average Speed: 28.85 Knots

Date	Lat. N.	Long. W.	Naut. Miles	Speed	Wind	Remarks
1969						
Nov. 2						Departure Havre L.V., 11:57 p.m., C.E.T.
Nov. 3	49-54	9-20	362	30.04	SW-7	Rough Sea, Moderate Swell
Nov. 4	48-33	29-22	789	30.94	N-5	Rough Sea, Low Swell
Nov. 5	43-57	47-22	796	31.21	NE-2	Slight Sea, Low Swell
Nov. 6	40-50	63-27	735	28.82	S-7	Rough Sea, Heavy Swell
Nov. 7			485	26.50	WNW-3	Arrived Ambrose L.S., 4:48 a.m., E.S.T.

Total Distance, LE HAVRE to NEW YORK: 3,167 Miles
Steaming Time: 4 Days, 10 Hours, 51 Minutes — Average Speed: 29.64 Knots

NOTE: A Nautical Mile is approximately 15 percent longer than a Statute or Land Mile

Prospective itinerary for the Grand Pacific cruise, 21 January 1970:

Lv New York	Wed 21 Jan	Noon
Ar Cristobal	Sat 24 Jan	pm
Transit Panama Canal	Sun 25 Jan	
Off Pitcairn Island	Sat 31 Jan	am
Lv Pitcairn Island	Sat 31 Jan	Noon
Ar Auckland	Thu 5 Feb	am
Lv Auckland	Fri 6 Feb	pm
Ar Wellington	Sun 8 Feb	am
Lv Wellington	Sun 8 Feb	pm
Ar Sydney	Tue 10 Feb	pm
Lv Sydney	Fri 13 Feb	pm
Ar Hong Kong	Fri 20 Feb	am
Lv Hong Kong	Sun 22 Feb	pm
Ar Kobe	Wed 25 Feb	am
Lv Kobe	Wed 25 Feb	pm
Ar Yokohama	Thu 26 Feb	am
Lv Yokohama	Fri 27 Feb	pm
Ar Honolulu	Wed 4 Mar	am
Lv Honolulu	Thu 5 Mar	am
Ar San Francisco	Sun 8 Mar	am
Lv San Francisco	Sun 8 Mar	pm
Ar Acapulco	Wed 11 Mar	am
Lv Acapulco	Thu 12 Mar	am
Off Balboa	Sat 14 Mar	am
Transit Panama Canal	Sat 14 Mar	
Ar New York	Tue 17 Mar	pm

Just before five in the morning on 7 November, the *United States*—the world's fastest ocean liner, the Blue Riband champion, the flagship of the entire American merchant marine—passed inbound off the Ambrose Lightship for the last time. Before eight, she was moored at Pier 86. In her seventeen years, she had logged 2,772,840 miles and carried 1,002,936 passengers on the North Atlantic and 22,755 on cruises. Soon, after a short trip to Newport News, her wheelhouse telegraph would read 'Finished with engines'.

Chapter 8

Virginia Limbo

The *United States* arrived at Pier 86, New York, just after daybreak on 7 November 1969. In short time, her last passengers went ashore, and then the final consignments of baggage and cargo. It was her last arrival at her home port.

Fred Rodriguez served aboard the *Big U* as a crew member on four of her final crossings, including Voyage No 400, the last trip.

By the fall of 1969, we had lost so many fine American passenger ships. Names like *America, Atlantic, Constitution, Independence* and more recently the *Brasil* and *Argentina* had become memories. It seemed, however, that the NMU [National Maritime Union] could always count on the *United States* arriving every two weeks and 'cleaning out' the Union hall with her needs for 1,000 crew. On 7 November I stayed aboard the liner to take some night photos from her bridge wing. Shortly before 8 pm, I made it up to the port wing and was busily snapping-away at various settings before the ship sailed for her scheduled drydocking period at Newport News. Suddenly, Commodore Alexanderson came out on the bridge and told me that I had to leave the ship immediately. Her sailing time had been advanced by an hour. He radioed to the last remaining gangway. But, quite fortunately, I was to go aboard one of the Moran tugs that would take the ship out. I made a run for it and just boarded the tug as the spring line was being cast off. Off we went and took up position on the port bow. The *United States* promptly let her lines go and, after sounding her mighty whistles, began backing out with the tugs pushing madly. I watched with complete amazement from the tug's fantail as the *United States*, all aglow in brilliant lights, swung around. All her cabin and deck lights were on, and her massive funnels lit as well. She looked like a birthday cake! Later, we picked up the docking pilot and away she went, sailing downriver ablaze in her lights. Little did I realize that it was to be the last time I would see her in service. A few days later, the front page of the second section of the *New York Times* ran the announcement of her withdrawal from service. Now, only the *Santa Rosa* and *Santa Paula* remained

in service—the last American liners out of New York—and even their days were numbered!

There were about 350 'skeleton' crew aboard the *United States* as she made the overnight run down to Virginia and most of them believed the official word out of 1 Broadway that she was to have her customary overhaul and would then return to service in time for the Christmas Caribbean cruise. Once at the shipyard, however, she went to a berth rather than directly into the big graving dock as was the custom. 'The refit began almost immediately,' recalled Leslie Barton, her last Chief Quartermaster. 'There was general and very thorough housecleaning underway on the 9th and the 10th. On the bridge, all the instruments were checked, the flags examined, the searchlights uncovered. The only difference this time was that MarAd [the Maritime Administration] was there as well. This was most unusual. An extreme and detailed inventory began, and even the clocks were being counted. Then, quite suddenly, when far from complete, the inspectors left. The orders were to go ashore.

'I went to the Executive Officer and he said that he had

Opposite Still majestic and regal, but faded, peeling, and in decay, the *United States* at her Norfolk berth. (*Fred Rodriguez*)

The port bridge wing from which, some twenty-five years earlier, the salutes of a Blue Riband winner had been received. (*Fred Rodriguez*)

A view from just above the starboard bridge wing. (*Fred Rodriguez*)

received a call from 1 Broadway. The ship was to be laid up. It was 11 November and everyone was to be off by 5 pm. Actually, some of us were permitted to stay a few extra days. All the flags were removed. Suddenly, the ship was dead.

'I stayed until the 14th. We had to check things out: six 7x50 binoculars, two forty-fives (guns) and six thirty-eights. These had to be taken ashore and delivered to MarAd. Two chronometers went also, and all the charts were placed in order and then rolled up and sent ashore. Six pairs of hand-cuffs went as well. The flags stayed in their lockers, however.

'Everyone was shaken up. I took one last thorough tour. She was desolate and lonely, but I could almost hear her talking: "It's not true, it's just not true!" I ran into others on board who were in tears. They'd lost their jobs, had no fami-lies, no future prospects. Many had left on that very day (the 11th) of the formal announcement. I left on the 14th, with a few others, and took only a suitcase and then went directly up to New York. We believed that the ship would return to service early in the new year and that only a

Christmas cruise would be cancelled. She was, after all, fully booked for the 17 January Great Pacific cruise. There was luggage already waiting on Pier 86. Instead, these passengers were reassigned to the *Leonardo Da Vinci*, which was also making a long cruise, a trip through Panama to Hawaii. I drove to Manhattan in a big Cadillac, but I was always very nervous in a car. Ironically, however, I wheeled the fastest liner on earth, one of the largest passenger liners ever built.

'After November 1969, the whole world seemed to collapse for me. Thirty-five years at sea all came to nothing. I never went back, never retrieved my personal effects or the closets full of uniforms. Later, I turned to bank work [in New York City]. I was, however, among the loyalist crewmembers who kept returning to the local union halls, thinking that the *United States* would be revived. The union leaders kept saying that she would!'

The sudden and startling news that the *United States* was to be laid up affected not only her 1,000 crewmembers and her future passengers, but also the dock crews on Pier 86 (which was left with only the Incres Line and its cruiseship, the *Victoria*, as a tenant), the United States Lines passenger departments and representatives in New York and throughout Europe as well, the provision and supply services, even the shipyard crews at Newport News. 'Simply, the new management at United States Lines [Walter Kidde & Co]

Below left Ladder in the ship's radar mast. (*Fred Rodriguez*)

Below The long neglected bow section. (*Fred Rodriguez*)

could make more money with cargo ships,' recalled Commodore Alexanderson. 'Liners were just not making a profit. By then [1969], the fleet had gone down from 55 ships to less than 30.

'I had gone home, on 12 November, after arriving at Newport News on the 8th. By the end of that week, I too had received the word from 1 Broadway. A week later, on Monday, the 16th, I returned to Newport News. The company suggested this. We were to lay off all crewmembers and deactivate the ship. All crew had to be paid off by Thanksgiving eve. Only two would remain: the chief engineer and I.

'We also had to take all provisions off. The stores were sent to a nearby United States Lines' freighter, the *American Legion*. We sold the liquor to one of the local officers' clubs. The foodstuffs were sent back to New York to be distributed to other ships of the line. Lots of cleaning had to be done as well. 4,000 tons of fuel oil were still aboard. The linens were sent to the linen lockers. Most of the crew belongings went with them, but others left things behind assuming that the lay up was only temporary. Mostly, these were never retrieved.

'The Chief Engineer and I were the only ones to stay aboard after Thanksgiving eve,' added the Commodore, 'but we lived ashore and had only a hot plate in the Commodore's pantry for lunch and for coffee. The ship grew colder. There was also shipyard security personnel aboard and a constant fire watch, but absolutely no visitors. Two months later [January 1970], a nearby ship was being sandblasted and all the grit blew onto the open decks of the *United States*. It fell on the sports and sun decks. The Chief Engineer and I rigged up several firehoses and together we washed-down the decks. Certainly, the situation was sad, but permanent. I wrote to a school, which had an adopt-a-ship programme, and which had adopted the *United States*, and told them that she was laid up. I recall also being interviewed by CBS News at the time. This too was sad—about the end, the end of the world's fastest ocean liner.

'By the spring, there was still no official news. There was very light communication with the Operations Department at 1 Broadway. It was not until May that I was told that I was going to a containership, the *American Legion*. I was recalled, however, in June, to move the *United States* to NIT (Norfolk International Terminal). It had become too expensive at Newport News what with berthing fees, security, fire watches, etc.

'Several locations were actually examined at the time, but NIT was finally selected. She was towed by tugs. There was

Opposite Looking aft from the starboard bridge wing. (*Fred Rodriguez*)

no power. She was tied up on a very hot, very humid day. The ship was stifling. There was no air-conditioning, of course. No one had been living on the *United States* for over six months.

'The United States Lines continued to pay all bills involving the ship until 1973, when she was officially transferred to MarAd. Soon after, MarAd contracted the Moon Engineering Co to install a dehumidification system on board. Thirteen big dehumidifiers were fitted and all exits were sealed except two, one aft and one forward. MarAd knew, of course, that continual dampness caused damage. These dehumidifiers took the moisture out of the ship. She was airtight.'

Little happened to the *United States* after her move to that long Norfolk finger pier, in June 1970. There were, of course, a small mountain of nostalgic magazine and newspaper articles mourning her glory days. There were also plenty of rumours about her future. There were all sorts of schemes for a new or revived career. There were reports, spread over several years, that she would become a rebuilt cruiseship, a stationary hotel, and then a motel, a conference centre, a floating condominium, a trade fair for industrial products, a museum ship, even a roving missionary centre. Among the most enticing items was a suggestion that she would be restored as a passenger liner, with occasional summertime transatlantic trips, and a ceremonious return to New York

Below From starboard aft, docking bridge wing. (*Fred Rodriguez*)

Below right Twin ports on the Boat Deck aft. (*Fred Rodriguez*)

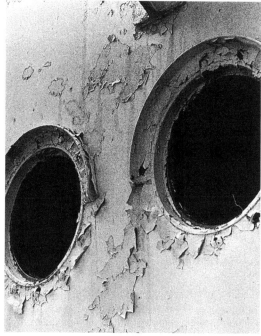

The Promenade Deck
aft. (*Fred Rodriguez*)

harbour on 4 July 1976, the nation's gala bicentennial. She would have been seen by tens of millions on television. But when those grand tall ships passed in review, surrounded by thousands of small boats in New York harbour, the *United States* was still at the same Norfolk berth—faded, rusting, lonely, far from any public attention, except for the two or three watchmen looking after her. There continued to be reports that she would be a world wide cruiseship: voyages to 'nowhere' and Bermuda, as well as periodic Atlantic crossings out of New York; Caribbean cruises from Miami; cruises to Hawaii, perhaps to Alaska from California, even one more long winter trip around the world. There were other schemes to make her a maritime museum at Norfolk, a floating casino-hotel at Atlantic City, a convention centre and hotel while berthed along a proposed rebuilt section of the New York City waterfront, at about West 34th Street, just a dozen or so blocks south of where she once regularly berthed.

The US Maritime Administration had taken full title of the *United States* in 1973. They paid $4.6 million in cash to the

Once there were boat drills and starch jacketed stewards, strolling passengers, and views of hypnotic ocean sunsets. The starboard Boat Deck in February 1986. (*Fred Rodriguez*)

United States Lines, who were only too happy to unload the burden of an idle 990-ft long ship. The United States Lines were unable to sell her themselves, however. There was a stipulation dating back to the time of her construction that specified that she could not be sold to foreign interests, nor to American concerns without government permission.

Realistically, there had been very little interest in the *United States* by foreign-flag passenger operators. The only recorded instance seems to have been in the late 1970s when the Norwegian-flag Kloster Group were looking for a large secondhand liner for conversion for their booming Caribbean cruise trades out of Miami. A Kloster team of management, engineers, and other technicians looked over the liner at Norfolk. They also looked at the idle Italian twins, *Michelangelo* and *Raffaello*, which had been decommissioned in 1975 and which were nested together at La Spezia south of Genoa. In 1977, they would be sold to the Shah of Iran's government, then in the throes of unbridled economic and military expansion, for use as floating barracks ships. But when the Kloster team went to the backwaters of Le Havre, once a bustling transatlantic liner port, to see the idle *France*, withdrawn in 1974, they were very impressed with the French flagship, in fact excited by her potential. She was slightly larger than the *United States* and the two Italian superliners, but—more importantly—her overall layout, configuration, and general design better suited Kloster's conversion plans. The *France* was purchased, in June 1979, for $18 million, and then sent off to the Hapag-Lloyd shipyards at Bremerhaven for a complete facelift costing $130 million (still less than building a comparable liner from scratch.) She re-emerged, in May 1970, as the stunningly restyled *Norway*. With her navy blue hull, with pools and rows of vinyl recliners now filling her upper decks, with two decks of shops, a disco named Dazzles, and even an ice cream parlour, she was then—and remains to date—one of the greatest and most successful conversions ever.

With continually rising shipbuilding costs, conversions of existing liners was a growing trend. The *United States* remained a candidate for conversion, especially in view of the

Another aft deck view that includes the once busy shuffleboard markings. (*Fred Rodriguez*)

marketing prospects of her illustrious heritage and her uniqueness as a US-flag liner in a cruise industry that sailed mostly out of American ports but in foreign-flag hulls. There had been precedents for converting existing liners that no doubt encouraged the Norwegians as well as other investors to investigate the conversion possibilities of the *United States*.

Carnival Cruise Lines had redone, although on a far more limited basis, Canadian Pacific's *Empress of Canada*, once on the transatlantic trade out of Liverpool, as the Caribbean cruiseship *Mardi Gras*. Later, that same Miami-based firm took the South African 'mailboat' *S. A. Vaal* and had her rebuilt as the *Festivale*, also intended for the tropics.

Following the *Norway*'s debut, there were still more liner conversions—and so more rumours regarding the 'strong' possibilities with the *United States*. Notably, the Italian sisterships *Galileo Galilei* and *Guglielmo Marconi*, two-class liners that had served on the old Australian migrant and tourist trades, were restyled; the former becoming the *Galileo* for Chandris Cruises of Greece, the latter being far more extravagantly altered as the *Costa Riviera* for Costa Cruises of Italy. Perhaps more relevant to the potential of the idle American superliner was the case of the Greek *Olympia*, a 23,000-tonner that had been sitting at anchor, rusting and decaying, for

A telescopic view of the ship's mast, but with the radar equipment long since removed and stored below. (*Fred Rodriguez*)

nearly eight years before she was bought by Finnish interests for restoration. The old Greek ship was cleaned, partially stripped, and then taken to a Hamburg shipyard where she was refitted, given a new, more contemporary external look, and even re-engined (diesels were far more efficient than her original, but long-neglected steam turbines). With a new identity, and under the operational banner of Commodore Cruises of Miami, she returned to active service in the summer of 1983 as the *Caribe I*. But what about the *United States*? Wasn't the world's fastest liner, the one-time pride of the American merchant fleet, a prime candidate for conversion as well? Evidently not. More rumours about her revival began to drift about, but she remained at that same Norfolk berth.

Earlier, in the mid-1970s, the Maritime Administration realized that the ship had military potential, as a troopship or even as a hospital ship. Studies had actually been done; reports had been written; revised blueprints drawn up; scale models had even been created to show the *United States* as

Twin kingposts frame the bridge section and the forward funnel. (*Fred Rodriguez*)

193

Deck chairs once lined this enclosed promenade deck. (*Fred Rodriguez*)

a military vessel. A 1983 report entitled 'USNS UNITED STATES' reads:

Today, the United States Navy has no hospital ship in its fleet, active or inactive. The last of six converted *Haven* class hospital ships built during the Second World War, the *Sanctuary*, were modified in 1971 to serve as a 'dependent support ship' for dependants of ships homeported in Piraeus, Greece. She was never sent to Greece, however, and was subsequently laid up in 1974. As a hospital ship during the Second World War and later off Vietnam, she had an operating capacity of approximately 300 beds. She contained beds stacked four high which made routine patient care very difficult.

Compared to the *Sanctuary*, the USNS *United States* will have roughly five times the number of beds (no more than two high), greater seakindliness, better stability and survivability, almost twice the speed, more extensive and efficient medical complex and definite care capability.

The conversion of the *United States* to a hospital ship is not projected to be as difficult as many of her existing facilities can be adapted easily to support hospital functions and her interior arrangements configured to the requirements of a hospital ship. Primary alterations will be the addition of a helicopter deck aft, a VERTREP deck forward of the bridge, and the modernization of the principal auxiliary systems such as HVAC, electrical, etc. Other major modifications will be the arrangement of the interior spaces required to suit a hospital layout.

When converted to a hospital ship, the *United States* will be the best in the world. She will have the speed to be highly mobile on short notice, a well-balanced and efficient medical complex, very good stability and safety, and be able to steam under the protection afforded to hospital ships under the Geneva Convention.

The USNS *United States* will provide worldwide medical support to the Rapid Deployment Joint Task Force and other US forces which are engaged in combat operations. Readily mobilized, she can be sent on short notice to areas where hostilities are imminent. Secondly, the USNS *United States*, as a hospital ship, can be dispatched to support international disaster relief abroad. After conversion, the *United States* is expected to provide these medical support roles for an active period of 20 years.

The ship will be able to provide complete medical care—from on-site emergency to recuperative care—for patients until they can be returned to active duty or evacuated back to the continental United States for further treatment. Design capability will be 1,600 beds, of which 120 are reserved for intensive care patients, and 18 operating rooms with a surge capability of 23. Additional support facilities include complete X-ray facilities, diagnostic laboratories and blood banks, dental facilities, optical laboratories, physical therapy, central sterile receiving area and a medical equipment repair facility. The USNS *United States* will be a complete self-contained hospital facility, able to operate while underway or at anchor.

While in combat or emergency zone, patients will be received primarily by helicopter at the aft landing area during daylight or at night. Additionally, casualties can be received from or discharged to boats through side ports simultaneously.

It was also rumoured that, following conversion, the hospital ship *United States* would be based in the Indian Ocean. The Defense Department in Washington wanted the ship and were ready to take title, but the Navy Department, who would operate her, felt differently. The government agen-

A few odd deckchairs and a lone table for ping-pong sadly fill out this view, looking aft, of the Promenade Deck. (*Fred Rodriguez*)

cies could never come to terms. The Navy thought that she would be too expensive, too impractical for their needs. And so, the military potential in the fastest ever liner withered away.

There were other reports that the government would place her in a Federal Reserve Fleet, probably the one nearby, in Virginia's James River. There was a problem of bridge clearance, however, and so it was reported that her top radar mast and her two funnels would have to be trimmed. By spring 1988, according to Anthony Schiavone, the superintendent of the 'idle fleet' in the James River, 'There have been at least half a dozen different studies done to bring the *United States* here. The most recent was about six months ago.'

At the same time, MarAd was trying to sell off the *United States*. Initially, in the mid-1970s, the minimum price was $12,000,000 with a 10 per cent deposit. The responses were less than encouraging. Meanwhile, the *United States* was herself costing money, even for minimal services and rent at her berth at Norfolk International Terminal. More and more, she was being treated like government surplus—like some old barracks or a well-used, battered metal desk. By July 1978, there had been five separate sets of bids offered to the MarAd offices. By then, the minimum price had dwindled to $5,000,000.

There was a flash of excitement during that same summer. The Svanholm Research Laboratories of Washington submitted a bid of $7,500,000. Unfortunately, hopes were soon thwarted when the firm failed to submit the required deposit. The second highest bid in that same summer was for $5,000,000, the minimum stipulated by MarAd, from a Seattle developer and entrepreneur, Richard Hadley. But his bid included a stipulation for a $25,000,000 government loan and a ten-year purchase financing package. The government rejected this. A third bid, placed at $3,200,000, came from a Mr Budike of Wallingford, Pennsylvania. But he too had stipulations: a two-year government operating subsidy! He was quickly refused.

Mr Hadley's interest in the idle liner did not diminish, however. Well into the following year (1979), his interest in the ship seemed to increase. He formed US Cruises Inc, with the express interest of restoring the liner as a cruiseship— under her well-known name as well as under the Stars and Stripes. Furthermore, amidst an increasingly competitive North American cruise industry, he wanted an unusual niche in the market, for the ship and so he and his assistants planned for the world's first 'condominium style, timeshare' cruiseship. The idea, so they felt, of time-sharing on

such an illustrious superliner would be unbeatable. Certainly, with no other serious contenders about, the government was interested. They wanted to sell the ship as soon as possible, and they gradually warmed to Mr Hadley and his plans.

In June 1979, along with Frank Braynard, then just beginning to write his own book (and make some further sketches) on the *United States*, I travelled to Norfolk for a visit to the liner that would soon be idle for a full decade. She stood—in solemn majesty—high out of the water, dwarfing the terminal rooftop. Her bow seemed more pointed than I remembered, somehow sharper, perhaps higher. On the starboard bow, the white lettering of the word *States* had been painted over. Momentarily, and with all the uncertainty and the rumours surrounding her, I thought that she was being renamed!

Those enormous funnels also caught my eye. The colours were faded, but the starboard sides far more so. I had heard a story that, in 1977, only half the funnels were freshly repainted. The story went that, being the twenty-fifth year since her completion, the Newport News Shipbuilding & Dry Dock Co wanted to bring some prized guests and stockholders around to see her. From the dockside in a chartered

The *United States* as seen from a passing freighter. (*Fred Rodriguez*)

A night view of the idle liner, in December 1982. (*Fred Rodriguez*)

bus, the shipyard wanted to improve the general view of the otherwise sad and neglected ship. And so, as the story concluded, the shipyard volunteered to paint the funnels, but only the port sides, those which their guests would see! (This, of course, wasn't true at all.)

In actuality, in the very first days of that last overhaul, in November 1969, work had just begun before word was flashed from New York to stop everything. The painters had begun work on the funnels, attending only to the port sides. Consequently, and even after a decade of neglect and changing weather, the funnels remained in two distinct shadings of red, white, and blue.

We boarded through one of the two gangways that linked the otherwise quiet and seemingly lifeless liner to shore. Her condition was, however, in no way as bad as one might have expected. There were no sinister smells, no visible evidences of deepening decay. Lighting, while reduced, was adequate. We walked through what always appeared to be 'miles' of corridors, which prompted momentary thoughts back to merrier times—of luggage and stewards bearing silver trays, of the Windsors and the Trumans. The stairwells were especially well lit and we made our way to the public rooms. Like schools and churches, these busy lounges without people looked sad and melancholy. They were meant to be used, to witness life and sound. Panels of frosted glass had turned murky, the stainless trims needed polishing, and those arc-shaped leatherette chairs in the ballroom seemed out of place, all huddled together. A copy of the *New York Times*,

dated 7 November 1969, was still lying on a glass-topped cocktail table. Oddly, it hadn't yellowed—even after ten years. A mounted sign announced, 'Bingo starting at 2 pm'. Stray glassware, sometimes turned on their sides, rested atop the long bar. In one foyer, hundreds of vacuum cleaners were lined in formation, like soldiers in drill review, awaiting their next call to duty. The staterooms were partially stripped: bare mattresses overturned and then canted, curtains gone, and all linens removed and stored elsewhere. The furnishings for U89, part of the old Duck Suite, had already been taken ashore, and then sent onwards to a sort of 'immortality' at the Smithsonian Institution in Washington.

There were only two remaining exit doors to the outer decks: one in the stern section and the other, as I recall it, at the base of that trim silver-coated radar mast atop the wheelhouse. A few seabirds had somehow managed to enter the long promenade decks and once there, trapped and unable to leave, had died. Their remains were scattered about in that now vacant space where deckchairs and the 4 o'clock tea trolleys had once been. The wheelhouse was stripped bare, seemingly down to the last clock and wheel. The doors to the bridge wings were sealed shut and covered over. Even the commodore's quarters seemed barren. All that remained on his day-room sofa was a painting of the liner in happier times by New York harbour artist Fred Rodriguez. Somehow it had been left aboard (and, happily, was later retrieved by the artist himself). The high spot of our tour, as Frank Braynard took notes and made hurried but still evocative sketches, were several remade cabins on the Main Deck. The original aluminium furniture, which often appeared stark, even severe, was brightened and enhanced by fresh coats of darker, more contemporary colours, mostly soothing dark browns. The new carpets, drapes, and bed coverings matched in similar tones. New lamps, a re-covered sofa, and fresh flowers made it all warmly inviting. This was part of United States Cruises scheme to revive the ship, but for special time-share condominium-style cruising. They felt there would be thousands who would want to invest. Realistically, there were very, very few. As we stepped ashore, on that

The great bow section. (*Fred Rodriguez*)

warm June afternoon in 1979, two rather elderly watch-men—the official keepers of the great ship—smiled, bid us farewell and then returned, with rapt interest, to the day-time quiz programme that appeared on the small screen of their Japanese television set. The sounds from that little imported box were the liveliest and loudest heard all day aboard the *United States*.

Richard Hadley and his United States Cruises remained interested in the liner and sale negotiations continued over into 1980. There was a close call, however, about the same time. 'She broke loose and began to move away from the dock at Norfolk,' recalled Commodore Alexanderson, by then retired but living nearby. 'The forward anchor chain, which had been connected to a bollard, let go. The shackle broke and the ship began to move away from the dock. The gangways fell into the water and the power and telephone lines snapped. Only the watch was aboard at the time. One of the supervisors of the Norfolk International Terminal saw her shifting and called me at 8 in the morning. I called the United States Cruise people and soon two Curtis Bay Tow-ing Co tugs were sent to bring the ship back alongside. Nor-shipco sent riggers to resecure the ship. After the ship was re-secured, she broke adrift again and the gangway went back into the water. There were extremely high winds. The *United States* is so high-sided that with the winds off the dock, it creates enormous pressure.'

The deal with Richard Hadley and his interests was almost finalized by early 1980, but they insisted on a final check in a drydock. 'Curtis Bay Towing were given the contract to move her,' remembered the Commodore. 'Four tugs were to be used, with one standing by. The move was actually delayed by a day because of bad weather. The winds were blowing too hard. Line handlers were specially hired at the Norfolk terminal. We had to be very careful. She was light and, as always, those big funnels were just like sails. She was towed out stern first, turned around, and then towed to Norshipco. It was a 2½-hour tow job. There was lots of local publicity and lots of spectators about. A helicopter was overhead for photography. People with shares in United States Cruises' condo-share plan were invited to make the trip. Later, of course, this plan failed, was abandoned, and the money of the few investors returned. Also, Newport News Shipyard was approached about doing this inspec-tion of the *United States*, but they were reluctant.

'At Norshipco, she was put in stern first so that her propellers and rudder could be examined more easily. The verdict: perfect condition! There was no work, however,

Opposite Commodore Alexanderson with his idle supership, in February 1970. (*Alexanderson Collection*)

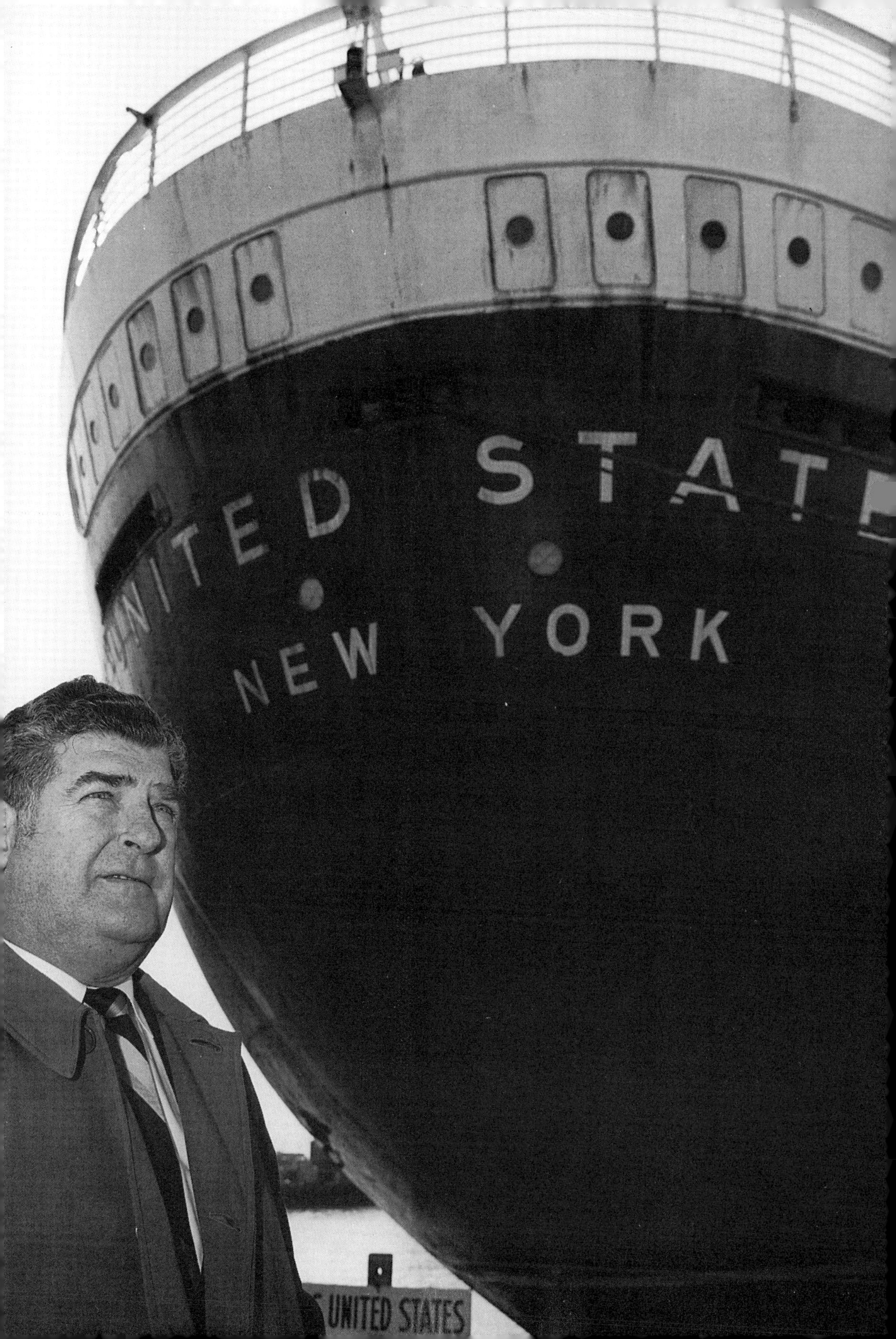
NEW YORK
UNITED STATES

other than the inspection and underwater examination. It took five days. Even the masses of oyster shells on the hull weren't removed. The underwater sections were also said to be in excellent condition, and even the paintwork was beyond expectations. The Redhand Paint Co, who were the suppliers in her United States Lines days, actually came down to Norfolk and took photos. After the five days, the *United States* was returned to her Norfolk berth, under tow and then re-secured. Lots of lines were used as well as anchor chains out to the bollards. There are also chains hanging on the outer side, both fore and aft; these are so she might be hauled away quickly in case of fire.

'Later, and after the ship was officially transferred to Hadley (and her homeport changed to Seattle), 3,000 of the 4,000 tons of Top Navy Grade Special fuel that had been left aboard in her tanks by United States Lines was taken out and sold. Normally, it was loaded at 110°F but it was taken out at only 65°F. Nicholas Bachko, who was one of the United States

An aerial view of the *United States* at the Norfolk International Terminal. (*Norshipco*)

Another aerial view, also dating from 1980. (*Norshipco*)

Lines' representatives at the shipyard when the ship was built and later was a consultant to Mr Hadley, arranged for the sale and transfer of the oil. He brought in Nicholas Landiak, a former First Assistant Engineer on the ship; Don Kadlac, a United States Lines port engineer; and William Van Cott and Emil "Brackie" Rauschenberg, both United States Lines engineers.'

Beginning in 1980, there seemed to be more constant rumours, odd announcements, even the occasional new story that—with financing of some $100 million, then up to $150 million, and finally up to $200 million in hand—the 'cruiseship' *United States* would be refitted and revived. The most persistent rumour for a time was that the ship would go first to Haiti, where all the cancer-causing asbestos would be removed; next, she would go to the Alabama Shipbuilding & Drydock Co at Mobile for structural work, including the addition of a new top sun-and-jogging deck; and finally that she would go to the HDW Shipyards at Hamburg for the final outfitting, redecorating, and the overall cosmetic change to a tropical, white-hulled cruiseship. None of these ever came to pass, mostly because of financial problems.

Among other details, a 1982 schedule was actually planned:

Date	Cruise
2 Jan	Los Angeles-Mexico-Honolulu (14 days)
16 Jan	Honolulu-Mexico-Los Angeles (14 days)

30 Jan	Los Angeles-Honolulu (14 days)
13 Feb	Honolulu-Los Angeles (14 days)
27 Feb	Los Angeles-Mexico-Honolulu (14 days)
13 Mar	Honolulu-Mexico-Los Angeles (14 days)
27 Mar	Los Angeles-Acapulco (7 days)
3 Apr	Acapulco-Los Angeles (7 days)
10 Apr	Los Angeles-Acapulco (7 days)
17 Apr	Acapulco-Los Angeles (7 days)
24 Apr	Los Angeles-Acapulco (7 days)
1 May	Acapulco-Los Angeles (7 days)
8 May	Los Angeles-Panama Canal-Miami (17 days)
25 May	Miami-Panama Canal-San Francisco (18 days)
12 Jun	San Francisco-Honolulu (14 days)
26 Jun	Honolulu-San Francisco (14 days)
10 Jul	San Francisco-Alaska-San Francisco (14 days)
24 Jul	San Francisco-Alaska-San Francisco (14 days)
7 Aug	San Francisco-Alaska-San Francisco (14 days)
21 Aug	San Francisco-Alaska-San Francisco (14 days)
4 Sep	Los Angeles-Honolulu (14 days)
18 Sep	Honolulu-Los Angeles (14 days)
2 Oct	Los Angeles-Panama Canal-Miami (17 days)

A broadside at
Norfolk, but more
recently — in 1988.
(*Frank J. Duffy*)

19 Oct	Miami-Panama Canal-Los Angeles (18 days)
6 Nov	Los Angeles-Acapulco (7 days)
13 Nov	Acapulco-Los Angeles (7 days)
20 Nov	Los Angeles-Acapulco (7 days)
27 Nov	Acapulco-Los Angeles (7 days)
4 Dec	DRYDOCK
18 Dec	Los Angeles-Hawaii-Mexico-Los Angeles (21 days)

But, once again, nothing came to pass. In October 1984, under the guise of stripping her in preparation for her refit, the Hadley interests authorized an auction—selling almost everything that was removable from the otherwise quiet and neglected liner. In fact, Hadley's project needed the money from such an auction, which would optimistically bring in as much as $5 million, just to pay off some of the ship's accumulated costs. After all, or so they and auctioneers, Guernsey's of New York City thought, there would be a near endless queue of aficionados and former passengers and staff who would want a piece, a choice memento, from the world's fastest liner.

The *Big U* in
Norshipco's floating
dock for survey, in
May 1980. The large
gas carrier *El Paso
Howard Boyd* is just
beyond the liner.
(*Norshipco*)

Over a decade's
growth on the aft
props. A view taken
in the Norshipco
drydock, May 1980.
(*Robert Russell*)

In all, over 12,000 visitors toured the ship at the time and,
among them, there were 3,000 actual bidders. Eagle-
embellished dinner plates, for example, sold for $1,100 per
dozen and later rose to $3,000 and then as much as $4,000.
Water glasses went for $25, blankets $25-50, and deckchairs
$65. The second highest sum paid was $17,000, for the bridge
fittings: two telegraphs, the radar, the main binnacle, and
two helmswheels. The highest amount, however, was for
the ship's bell.

In the spring of 1988, the author visited the Windmill Point
Restaurant in, of all places, Nags Head on North Carolina's
Outer Banks. The restaurant houses the largest collection
of items from the *United States* auction held over three years
before—the upper floor was even called the '*United States*
Lounge'. The centrepiece is the 20-ft long kidney-shaped bar
from the ship's first-class ballroom. Surrounding it are lamps,

chairs, leather sofas, framed posters, and menu cards, even the stainless railings from the balcony in the first-class restaurant. On one chair, I noticed markings indicating that it had been re-upholstered during Voyage 364, in 1967, just two years before the ship's decommissioning. Several large framed photos of the ship were especially evocative. The most impressive was an aerial departure scene from New York's Pier 86, with crowds along the outer decks and on the pier's far-end balcony, and another of a streamer-filled departure from Southampton's Ocean Terminal. Ironically, both structures are now gone as well, victims of demolition crews.

The restaurant is owned by Dr Sarah E. Forbes, an endlessly energetic and wonderfully enthusiastic collector. Although she never sailed aboard the *United States*, she is devoted to what was America's finest ocean liner. 'I was torn apart by the destruction of the *United States* when almost every removable piece of her was put up for auction. After all, beauty is the interaction of creative abilities, the purer craftmanship of it all. The planning, the construction—it was pure genius. Somehow, we have not surpassed this in our atomic-computer age. Advanced technical skills have not surpassed the building of this great ship.

'When I heard of the auction, I felt a great sadness. I didn't like the breakup of so much of that fine ship and so I purchased $300,000 worth of objects: tables, chairs, artwork. I was especially disappointed, however, to find that the ship's bell had already been sold. But, fortunately for me, the buyers could not complete the financing and so, for $32,000, I bought it. Earlier, I had purchased a gift shop property

The *United States* lives on: her forward whistle at its new home in Massachusetts under the care of her present owner.

at Nags Head and decided to convert it into a restaurant. Using the items from the *United States* seemed perfect. The pieces could be used as well as seen. Gradually, the chairs and tables and other fittings were sent from Norfolk by truck. The first-class ballroom bar was perhaps the most difficult. It had to be lifted by a specially hired crane to an opening cut in a second-floor wall!'

The ground-floor lobby of the restaurant includes the restored 400 lb bell as well as a 4-ft long model of the ship, one which had been stored in a cargo hold on board and which now has been painstakingly restored. Nearby, in the actual restaurant section, all of the tables and chairs from the first-class restaurant are in use. Included in these are the larger tables once used by the Commodore and the Chief Engineer.

Dr Forbes has more items, including one of the ship's builders' plates, in storage and plans to use them as the restaurant expands. In the Windmill Point Restaurant, the *United States* seems to live on. Other items have also found further use. One Massachusetts businessman bought the whistle from the ship's forward funnel which had been stored in one of the forward holds since 1973. In May 1988, he reported, 'We have used the whistle on special occasions, using compressed air.' Again, the *United States* lives on.

All sorts of items from the liner continue to circulate, mainly through flea markets and antique shops, but mostly through the increasingly brisk business of maritime memorabilia. Kenneth Schultz, from Hoboken, New Jersey, perhaps the best-known ocean liner collectibles dealer, bought considerable amounts from the *United States* auction. These were later offered for sale through his extensive catalogues: menu cards at $5, 1952 vintage deck plans at $25, stateroom bath mats at $45. In all, there were 160 pieces of *United States* memorabilia in his November 1987 catalogue. Item No 726, however, was perhaps the most intriguing, certainly one of the most costly, and was, as Mr Schultz put it, 'a spectacular item'. The description read:

20″ x 12″ builders plate of solid bronze with a black face and silvered lettering and weighing 28 lbs. Raised out letters read:

UNITED STATES
N.N. Hull No. 488
Maritime Commission No. 2917
Newport News Shipbuilding & Dry Dock Company
1952
Price: $5,000

Yet, despite her continued solitary idleness and sad neglect at Norfolk, the *United States* continues to live on.

Chapter 9

The Cruiseship
United States

The *United States* would have made a fascinating cruiseship conversion. Externally, she would probably have seemed longer—that long, low hull painted completely white, the anchors highlighted in black and twin stripes of red and blue added just below the promenade deck windows. Just below the position of the former forward cargo hold, a large blue eagle would be painted on each side and the stripes reworked to a single red and double blue. The radar mast atop the bridge would have been in white to match the overall colour of those twin massive funnels. But the forward sections of each stack would now be striped in vertical strips of a narrow red and then a much wider blue. The blue would have run over the tops of the funnels and onto the smoke-deflecting fins. In fact, the new colours for United States Cruises would have been a variation on the horizontal red, white, and blue colouring of the United States Lines. The kingposts and booms would have been removed (she would no longer carry any cargo whatsoever and therefore wouldn't need them) and at least two large tenders would be mounted amongst the other white-painted lifeboats.

A new top deck would have been added and one would have included an additional 102 cabins, and so begins an imaginative prospectus about the 'new' *United States* as planned by her current owners.

'High above the sea, the new Eagle Deck is the top deck of the vessel. Forward is the spectacular Eagle's Nest Lounge, commanding an unmatched view of the vessel's course. Extensive use of glass makes the outside world passing by part of the Eagle's Nest. Aft of the Eagle's Nest Lounge, the creation of these new staterooms offers a variety of open deck space, over 35,000 square feet. A unique feature of this deck is the new oval sunwalk. Both the sunbathing and promenading passenger are offered unparalleled views of the seascape. Extensive use of new wooden deck cover-

213

ing and a high glass wind screen around the perimeter creates an atmosphere for topside activities second to none. On both starboard and port sides is an open promenade running the length of the 560-ft deck and in between is an ample running track. This track is utilized both for scheduled and unscheduled passenger jogging, "walk-a-thons", and other events. Two supervised competition-sized tennis courts with professionally supervised instruction is found between the open promenades on this deck. The aft part of the Eagle Deck provides a panoramic view of sea and sky and overlooks the lower decks and pool areas.

'The navigational bridge is forward on the Vista Deck (formerly the Navigation Deck). This deck has been extended aft and the 102 new deluxe staterooms added (including six lanai suites, aft, each with its own private terrace). Seventy-four deluxe outside doubles on this deck offer a panoramic ocean view from their large square windows. Twenty-two deluxe inside doubles complete the staterooms on this deck.

'The Lanai Deck (formerly the Sports Deck) provides primarily for the Master and Officers' accommodations. In addition, there are eight passenger staterooms. Passenger facilities on this deck include two racquetball courts and a court lounge as well as pet kennels, complete with a kennel attendant. Located aft is Independence Square—6,000 square feet of open-air lounge connecting directly to 8,000 square feet of sun deck and promenade over the Hibiscus Pool. Main event themes for each day begin with special lunches held in this area. There will be "Wild West Days" with "hoedown" music; "Aloha Luau" lunches with music of the Hawaiian Islands; "Heritage Days" with European lunch specialities and folk music; "Americana Day" with hot dogs, hamburgers and apple pie; and a "Fourth of July" celebration on every cruise, regardless of the day or month.

'The Sun Deck accommodates 110 elegantly appointed staterooms, 37 of which are totally new. Completely surrounding the staterooms is an open promenade, perfect for strolling in the fresh air or relaxing in a deck chair in the shade. The aft portion of this deck leads to one of the most dramatic transformations of the vessel. The architect and his interior designers have created the Raintree Lounge, a two-storey garden with glass walls, a curved glass ceiling and access from the Promenade Deck by four glistening elliptical stairways. Looking out from this exciting room, the passenger has a superlative 300-degree view of the sea as well as the protected view of the Hibiscus Pool. This beautiful pool, which resembles a four-leaf clover, is enhanced by a cascading fountain sculpture in its centre. This pool is the site of daily "splash" parties.

'While the original Promenade Deck was designed to protect the transatlantic passenger from the adverse elements of the North Atlantic, the concept for the new United States is broader and offers the discriminating passenger an array of stimulating experiences. Leaving the forward foyer and strolling aft on the new Promenade Deck, passengers are confronted with a dazzling amount of activity, sights and smells. Passing the Grand Ballroom, travellers can listen to the best orchestra dance music and even catch a glimpse of famous etched glass panels with their elusive and subtle mermaids. At this point, there is a choice of the all-new Palm Bar and the crystal display of glass and spirits or the refreshing sidewalk cafes, Friday's and Le Bistro, presenting deli and café delicacies along with the world's greatest coffees, chocolates and pastries. Further along the Promenade Deck is the Vegas Room for those passengers who may wish to engage in a game of chance. Architecturally enhanced by the all-new Showplace America, the ship's original theatre now serves as the centre of formal entertainment for all passengers and featuring cabaret-style entertainment as well as first-run films. For after-the-show drinks, the lower entrance to the Raintree Lounge is conveniently located directly aft of Showplace America. Located forward on the Promenade Deck are the Seminar Theatre and the Heritage and Colony lounges, in which are found the library, writing room, reading room and chapel. Quiet and secluded from the activity of the rest of the Promenade Deck, these areas are used for various daytime activities such as the Ladies Sewing Circle, the Conversation Circle and costume-making for the Masquerade Ball.

'The Aloha Deck (formerly the Upper Deck) is devoted primarily to staterooms. There are six luxurious three-room Admiral's suites and 160 staterooms. Further aft on the Aloha Deck are the children's playroom/nursery, a sundries shop, electronic game room and the all-new Plantation Lounge. This light and airy space, reminiscent of a classic south seas plantation manor house, is the setting for an all-day poolside lounge featuring a lavish breakfast-brunch buffet. During the day, light snacks and beverages are available. The pace is relaxed and the elegant rattan furniture is soft and comfortable. Potted palms and window shutters set the mood for this Plantation Room at sea. The focal point of this area is the oval-shaped Dolphin Pool, located further aft. Curving stairs on either side of the pool provide easy access to the novel sunwalk above.

'Below the Plantation Lounge, on the Bahamas Deck (formerly the Main Deck) is another one of the most exciting shipboard lounges at sea. In the spirit of Fitzgerald's lavish New York society lawn parties, Gatsby's Lounge captures a festive party mood. This elegant saloon with its rich veneer wood, brass detailing, accents of crystal and bevelled mirrors at the bar, features a striking "pressed tin" ceiling. Of course, no classic saloon would be complete without a shiny brass rail and Gatsby's is no exception; its brass bar rail, held in place by a dozen Indian elephants with curving tusks and trunks, rivals any on land or sea. The Bahamas Deck also includes two conference rooms, the reservations centres, information desk, travel office, bank, baggage office and 177 staterooms. The grand staircase to the Blue Riband dining-room one deck below is located here as well.

'Five of the ship's seven new restaurants are located on the Catalina Deck (formerly A Deck). Unlike other cruiseships which have assigned dining, each passenger on the *United States* may choose his or her individual dining preference and dinner companions. The themes selected by the designers offer the best of decor for gourmet dining. Prominently featured and centrally located mid-ship is the luxurious and exciting Blue Riband dining-room, offering continental cuisine and invitational formal dining with the ship's captain and other officers. The sophisticated high fashion design of Gauguin's and the Portofino restaurants, located aft of the Blue Riband, provides the appropriate setting for continental entrees and accoutrements featured in these restaurants. For less formal but still excellent dining, the South Seas restaurant offers a wide variety of speciality gourmet treats from curries and egg rolls to sweet, slowly roasted Polynesian pork. Also on the informal side is London's, presenting the best of the world's grills from prime steak to lobster tails. Both of these restaurants are located forward of the Blue Riband on this deck. In addition to the dining facilities are 113 staterooms, crew quarters and the first glimpse of the ship's shopping centre. In total, nearly one-half acre of boutiques and shops are located on three decks in the stern of the ship and offers the best and most beautiful from all over the world. Over 4,000 square feet are located on the Catalina Deck. A new elevator provides access to the additional shops located immediately below on the Discovery and Empire decks.

'Formerly B Deck, the Discovery Deck houses over 8,000 square feet of shopping space and includes a men's shop and a ladies' boutique, both featuring the latest in designer fashions and accessories; a jewellery store with fine china, sterling silver and crystal; a bookstore; drug store; and more. In addition to 108 staterooms and crew quarters is the hospital and dispensary, which are located forward on this deck.

'An additional 6,000 square feet of shopping facilities are found directly on the Empire Deck (formerly C Deck), and just forward is the indoor swimming pool and gymnasium. Fully equipped with a Universal Gym, leg curl machine, double chest machine, rowing machine, sit-up boards and exercise bicycles, the gym will also be complemented with a sauna, steam bath and massage facilities. The remainder of the deck is devoted to crew quarters, cold storage, operational machinery and engine spaces.

'D and E decks contain additional crew quarters, support facilities and operational equipment and machinery. They are not accessible to cruise passengers, except by escorted tour.'

What an exciting cruise liner the 'new' SS *United States* would be!

Epilogue

My last visit to the *United States* was on a November day in 1987. My guide was none other than Commodore Leroy Alexanderson, the last master of the great liner. As we approached the berth by car, I realized all over again just how large she is—the enormous hull section sitting rather high in the water (and secured fore and aft by dozens of ropes), the raked funnels (in increasingly faded hues of red, white, and blue, and with her once thunderous whistles now removed), the long white superstructure, and the neatly set rows of two dozen silver lifeboats (the paintwork is peeling so badly that it has begun to curl and layers are dropping off). Otherwise, the setting—on that gusty autumn afternoon—was desolate and lonely.

There was considerable debris along the dockside: battered metal furniture such as chests of drawers, chairs and cabinets. Two gangways led to the ship and one of these led into the cramped, chilly, and generally uninviting 'official entrance' on B Deck. This ill-kept reception area was merely a prelude to the ship's condition. Several run-down, disorganized desks seemed to serve as the ship's nerve centre. Musty United States Lines' blankets were strung-up as partitions across the ship's passageways, which seemed colder and darker and more uninviting still.

Once in the passenger areas, there was barely any light, either natural or artificial. Fortunately, the Commodore, who had served aboard the ship since 1955 until her retirement fourteen years later, knows his way about the labyrinth of corridors and stairwells and those rarely seen crew passages. He led the way and together we were guided by his flashlight. When I last visited the *United States*, in June 1979, she was in almost perfect condition, even if she had already been idle for nearly a decade. Then, she had a definite sense of order and most of her furnishings were still on board. But on this visit, the scene was very different. There was litter and debris everywhere—or so it seemed. All the furniture, artwork, and decorations seemed to be gone, mostly sent ashore after being sold at auction. All the doors, even from the stateroom closets, were gone. Most of the plumbing fixtures had been taken away as well.

We stopped at Cabin U89, part of the suite complex that was always occupied by the Duke and Duchess of Windsor, and found that even part of the wall covering had been cut out. The long white tub where the Duchess had once bathed was now filled with dirt and scraps. All the handrails, even on the stairwells, had been removed. Scattered about were piles of soiled linens, broken chairs and tables, greasy cables, wires and ropes. Water leakage had begun along the aft upper decks. Some of the promenade windows were cracked, others broken completely; the enclosed promenade area was littered with several grim layers of dead birds. The long tubes of the elaborate dehumidification system (installed by the Federal Government in 1973 and which all but kept the liner airtight until 1980) had been disconnected and, in places, released and sent crashing down along the darkened corridors. A yellowing bingo notice was still posted in one lounge and another advertised 'photos for sale, $1'. I found some telephone directories in the ship's travel office, including one for Hoboken, New Jersey, dated 1958-9, which contained listings for several members of my family. It was a very sad, discouraging, and sentimental visit.

There was recurring talk at this time that the *United States* and her Seattle owners would soon have to find an alternative berth. After nineteen years at the same Norfolk berth, the 990-ft long liner was to face yet another indignity: eviction. Legal actions by the owners of the Norfolk International Terminal had evidently been in process for some time. It seems that the space was now needed for cargo ships. After some delays, an alternative berth was finally found at the CSX coal pier at nearby Newport News, her birthplace. Amidst all of this were rumours that she would soon leave for Tampico in Mexico, where she would be stripped of her asbestos, and then go to the Avondale Shipyards in New Orleans for the first major phase of her renewal as a cruiseship.

William A. Fox, a naval architect and ardent fan of the *Big U*, wrote a detailed chronicle of the shift in the Autumn 1989 edition of *Steamboat Bill*: 'Her long delayed move was intended for Tuesday, February 28th [1989], but incomplete preparations at Newport News and miserable weather conditions made that impossible. The move was not possible

for three days because of the placement of a tube for the new
I-664 bridge-tunnel across the James River. So, Saturday,
March 4th, became moving day.'

tube for the new I-664 bridge-tunnel across the James River.
So, Saturday, March 4th, became moving day.'

The shifting of the idle liner required six tugs. 'We arrived
at NIT Pier 2 at 8:30 in the morning,' according to Bill Fox,
'and the familiar shape of the *United States* loomed out of
the fog. She was riding light, with a draft of 22 ft forward
and 25 ft aft. Her paint was peeling and she was rusting,
but she was still a powerful beauty. A furled American flag
hung on her ensign staff. Commodore Alexanderson later
joined our press party aboard the tug *Nancy McAllister*.

'We expected to wait an hour but, like the planned renovation of the big ship, things were not destined to happen
quickly. The problem was the lines, which were nearly
impossible to handle with a small crew and a single winch
fed by shore power. The first line to go was a chain to the
bow, and it had to be burned off. Communications between
the ship and the pier were a major problem, and the old
lines were tangled and fouled with gear. There was a four-
hour delay.

'The afternoon dragged on and the weather got worse. As
2:00 pm approached, the final lines were freed and we were
ready to get underway. At 2:05, the tugs went to work and
the *United States* slowly began to move away from the pier.
It was an unexpected and emotional instant, and I had a
momentary feeling that the *United States* was sailing for Le
Havre, not simply being towed to Newport News.

'With the tugs deployed as planned, we entered Norfolk
Harbor Reach and soon were moving northward at about
6 knots. Due to the fog not much could be seen, but the
picture along the ship's bow from the tug's wheelhouse was
spectacular. A slight wake suggested that the ship was towing us, not vice-versa. Our new nylon hawser stretched and
set up a racket, and those on deck kept their distance from
it. By 3:00 pm, we had arrived at Buoy No 7, and began the
135-degree port turn into the Newport News Channel. An
hour later, we rounded Newport News Point and the big
ship entered the James, river of her birth, for the first time
in nearly twenty years.

'The evening news carried the story, with interviews, aer-
ials from helicopters and vintage footage. They did a superb
job. The *United States* again made the front page the next
morning under the headline "Glimpse of Liner Worth the
Wait". United Press International ran a photo which was cap-
tioned "Misty Memories". It had been a splendid event and

a time of intense local pride, and everyone thought that the story was over for a while.

'This was not to be, as the liner was in the news again on Tuesday (March 7th). On Monday night, in 40 mph winds, she broke loose from her moorings and made an unscheduled dash for freedom. Her old fibre lines had parted and a steel bow line had held but tore a cleat from the pier. Her bow swung about a quarter mile before she struck adjacent Pier 14 and came to a halt. Nearby McAllister Towing again came to her assistance, moved her back to Pier 15, and held her there through the night. Undamaged, she was re-moored with difficulty on Tuesday, since her shore power connections had been severed and the lines had to be worked by hand. McAllister stayed with her Tuesday night, and left only when the storm finally abated.

'On Thursday, an editorial ran in the *Daily Press*. Entitled "Worse than Death", it lamented her fate and suggested that she had been trying to break loose in order to reach the Atlantic and a dignified end to her career.'

Still a sad and lonely ship, she now seems only to be the subject of continuing rumours: that despite all the odds, she will finally become an active cruiseship, though perhaps with 'overseas' financing; that she will be scrapped; that she will be resold to the government and then sent to the nearby James River reserve fleet; that, at the prompting of some devoted and financially sound loyalists, she will be enshrined as a museum and entertainment centre—the East Coast version of the *Queen Mary* on the West Coast; and finally that real estate multi-millionaire Donald Trump should buy her for use as a floating hotel and casino.

But there is one point that remains certain: more will surely be written in the story of the world's fastest ocean liner, the last Blue Riband champion* and former pride of the entire American merchant marine: the SS *United States*.

---

*In June 1990, the largest commercial catamaran ever built, the 3,000 gross ton *Hoverspeed Great Britain*, which is part of a planned quartet also known as *Hoverspeed Sea Cat*, set off on an Atlantic crossing. Built in Tasmania and owned by Sea Containers Ltd of London (but registered in the Bahamas), her operational purpose is to cut cross-Channel travel time in half — to 2 hours 40 minutes for the run between Portsmouth and Cherbourg.

In crossing the North Atlantic, this initial *Sea Cat* shaved 2 hours 46 minutes off the record set by the *United States* some 38 years earlier. A Blue Riband Committee was re-established and, from the start, favoured the new catamaran. The guardians of the Hales Trophy on behalf of the now defunct United States Lines were the American Merchant Marine Museum; resistant at first, the Museum eventually accepted the Committee's decree, that the *Sea Cat* was the new Blue Riband holder and the world's fastest commercial passenger craft. The trophy departed American shores in October.

Bibliography

Armstrong, Warren. *Atlantic Highway* London: George G. Harrap & Co Ltd, 1961).

Billings, Henry. *Superliner SS* United States (New York: Viking Press, 1954).

Bonsor, N.R.P *North Atlantic Seaway,* (Prescot, Lancashire: T. Stephenson & Sons Ltd, 1955).

Braynard, Frank O. *By Their Works Ye shall Know Them* (New York: Gibbs & Cox Co, 1968).

—— *The Big Ship: The Story of the SS* United States (Newport News, Virginia: Mariners Museum, 1981).

Coleman, Terry. *The Liners* (New York: G. P. Putnam's Sons, 1977).

Crowdy, Michael (ed.). *Marine News* (1964—89) (Kendal, Cumbria: World Ship Society).

Devol, George (ed.). *Ocean and Cruise News* (1980—9) (Stamford, Connecticut: World Ocean & Cruise Society).

Dunn, Laurence. *Passenger Liners* (Southampton: Adlard Coles Ltd, 1961).

Eisele, Peter (ed.). *Steamboat Bill* (1966-89) (New York: Steamship Historical Society of America Inc.).

Kludas, Arnold. *Great Passenger Ships of the World,* volumes 1—5 (Cambridge, England: Patrick Stephens Ltd, 1972—6).

Watson, Milton. *US Passenger Liners Since 1945* (Wellingborough, Northamptonshire: Patrick Stephens Ltd, 1988).

Index